Late-Talking Children

Late-Talking Children

Thomas Sowell

BasicBooks
A Division of HarperCollins*Publishers*

Copyright © 1997 by Thomas Sowell.

Published by BasicBooks, A Division of HarperCollins Publishers, Inc.

FIRST EDITION

Designed by Laura Lindgren

Library of Congress Cataloging-in-Publication Data

Sowell, Thomas, 1930–
    Late-talking children / Thomas Sowell.—1st ed.
        p. cm.
    Includes bibliographical references and index.
    ISBN 0-465-03834-4
    1. Interpersonal communication in children.   2. Children—
Language.   3. Psycholinguistics.   4. Language acquisition—Parent
participation.   5. Slow learning children.   I. Title.
    BF723.C57S68   1997
    649'.68—dc21   97-3412
                                                                        CIP

97 98 99 00 01 ❖/RRD 10 9 8 7 6 5 4 3 2 1

To my son, John, who was late in talking but early in thinking

CONTENTS

ACKNOWLEDGMENT

A debt of gratitude is owed, first of all, to the dozens of parents of late-talking children who shared their stories with me and who filled out long questionnaires about their children's development and family background for this study. Dr. Rita Steele, a psychologist in private practice, generously gave of her time to determine what she could about some of the children in our group. Numerous academic specialists in various fields offered me help in locating individuals, institutions, and literature that might aid in trying to understand why bright children were talking late. So did Heather Richardson Higgins of the Randolph Foundation, who helped me spread a net far and wide for people with expertise in related areas. My assistant, Na Liu, has as usual not only helped by assembling and tabulating material for this book (including catching my errors), but also by taking care of all the other things that might otherwise distract me from it. A very special debt of gratitude is owed to Professor Steven Pinker, Director of the Center for Cognitive Neurosciences at M.I.T., who not only searched the literature for me but generously offered information and suggestions which proved to be invaluable. Ms. Christine Lim of M.I.T. was also very helpful in supplying me with an annotated bibliography on speech problems and brain functions.

None of these people shares any responsibility for the

shortcomings of this book, especially since I, like many of the children in our group, was headstrong enough to go my own way in the end.

THOMAS SOWELL
Hoover Institution

· one ·

A Personal Experience

WITH SO MUCH SCIENTIFIC AND MEDICAL LITERATURE ALREADY available on late-talking children, why would anyone write another book about them—especially someone who has no pretensions to scientific or medical expertise?

While much has been written about children who talk late, and about the many other serious problems they often have, there is virtually nothing written about the special kind of child who talks late but who otherwise shows at least normal, and often above-normal, intelligence in other ways. I am the father of such a child. When I first wrote about him in a newspaper column, after he graduated from college with a degree in computer science, letters began to come in from around the country from parents and grandparents of similar children.

After their children passed their second, third, or even fourth birthday without talking, most of these parents took them to be tested for all sorts of things. Most of these tests turned up nothing wrong—and often the experts seemed as baffled and frustrated as everyone else. Some non-verbal intelligence tests showed that some of these children could do things that most other children their age could not do. In at least one case, the child could do things that the person administering the test could not do, but the tester knew that the child's answers were right because the correct answers had been supplied with the test.

There was something else unusual about these children. The first 30 I heard about were all boys. The odds against that happening by random chance are astronomical. At various times in my life, I have personally encountered some late talkers who turned out fine—six altogether, besides my son—and all of these were boys as well. One was my friend and fellow-economist Professor Walter Williams of George Mason University. Not all late talkers have been male, however. Highly intelligent female late talkers include distinguished mathematician Julia Robinson. Nuclear physicists who talked late include Richard Feynman, Edward Teller, and Albert Einstein.

There have been many labels applied to these children. In fact, these labels have been a major problem and a major source of anguish to their parents. Some observers—neighbors, relatives, teachers—have regarded these children as simply "retarded," but there are also other and more scientific-sounding labels like "pervasive developmental disorder" or—the most dreaded of all—"autistic." There are some children to whom such labels legitimately apply, so I did not want to give these parents (or other parents) false hopes. But it also became clear that such labels were sometimes used when there was neither sufficient evidence for them as regards the particular child nor sufficient professional qualifications by the person applying the label, or both.

Many of the parents who wrote me were hoping that I could either give them scientific or medical explanations of what was happening or perhaps some practical advice on how to get their children talking, or how to improve whatever talking they were doing. I could do none of these things, but I tried to find something that might be helpful to these parents in the scientific, medical or psychological literature. After my efforts and the efforts of my research assistant to find something that might be useful to these parents failed, I decided instead simply to tell them that I had come up empty and ask if they would be interested in being put in touch with each other. Most accepted my offer to help them form a group to communicate with one another by mail or phone, and seemed much relieved just to be able to end their sense of utter isolation and be able to talk with someone else who could understand their situation.

Particularly valuable as sources of personal experience were five mothers whose sons had already grown up and were doing fine. After a while, the parents in the group began circulating letters among themselves and sending me copies. These letters contained some remarkable stories. This book will share some of those stories. Let me begin, however, with my own story—or rather, the story of my son.

———————

John was born somewhat prematurely but otherwise was a normal baby. At least we thought of him as normal until the years began to pass without his talking. When he wanted something, he would point to it. When he was hungry, he would pat the refrigerator so that we would open it up, and then he would point to whatever he wanted to eat or drink.

During this period, we lived in an upstairs duplex apartment in a housing complex in Ithaca, New York, where I taught at Cornell University. There were many other young academics like ourselves there, beginning their families. We became particularly self-conscious when other children, born since we moved in when John was six months old, began to talk while John still said nothing.

Somewhere around his third year he began to say an occasional isolated word. "Rocky" he liked to cry out when he heard newscaster Frank Blair on the "Today" show say what the weather was like west of the Rockies. And when John saw a body of water—a pond, a lake or a river—he would cry out "wah-ee." There were a few other words he would say, but they were all used in isolation and not to accomplish any practical purpose nor to communicate some thought or feeling. Moreover, even in the case of water, he used "wah-ee" only for bodies of water, not for water in a glass or water coming out of a faucet. He apparently saw no connection between the water he drank and the water he saw in waterfalls, ponds and other places.

Despite not talking, John gave other signs of understanding. I could tell him to go into his room and get the red pillow and bring it to me—and he would do so immediately. He even developed a dangerous ability to open the child locks we had on the grates we put across the kitchen door and across an open stairwell in our upstairs duplex apartment. I had to buy more complicated child locks to keep him from dangerous places. He was not yet walking, but was sitting in his little walker one day when I noticed him looking intently at a new child lock I had bought to put on the grate across the kitchen door. He did not attempt to open it by trial and error, but just stared at it closely for a very long time, without touching it. Then he reached out and opened it on the first try.

We used our most complicated child lock on the grate protecting John from the open stairwell. One day, when we were not looking, John figured out that lock as well—and went tumbling down the long flight of stairs, still in his walker, because he was not yet old enough to walk. He cried out in hurt and fright but, fortunately, he was not injured.

After John began to walk, he began to explore and to analyze things, though we of course had few clues as to what was going on in his mind. One pattern, however, he repeated on a number of occasions. There was a door in the living room that led out to a tiny balcony. On warm days, we would leave the door ajar to let in some fresh air. As the sunlight struck a glass pane in the door, it would reflect off onto the opposite wall of the living room where the pattern of latticework in the door would appear. John became fascinated with this.

He would go over to the door, examine it closely, then run across the room to the wall and examine the reflection. Then he would go back to the door and change the angle very slightly and run back to the reflection again to see if it had moved. Then he would go back and change the angle again and come back to see how the reflection had moved. He did this on so many occasions that one day I decided to photograph it. I still have the slide showing John looking up at the reflection with a smile of fascination. He was so young that he still had a pacifier hanging around his neck. Yet he wasn't talking and it would be years before he would talk.

One day, when John was about three, a televised speech by President Lyndon Johnson was preceded by a picture of the presidential seal that filled the TV screen. John immediately ran back into his room and returned with one of the Kennedy half-dollars that his grandmother had given him. He then compared the presidential seal on the screen with the presidential seal on the back of his Kennedy half-dollar.

There were other indications of his memory. I liked to take John to a park on the opposite side of Cayuga Lake from where we lived. During the long winter months we did not go there but, when the weather became good in the spring, I decided one day to take him back again. As you drive along the highway on that side of the lake, there is a long stretch where you cannot see the water. But, as we came around a bend—just before the lake came into view—John cried out "wah-ee"! He knew we had reached the point where we were about to see the lake.

Perhaps the most remarkable example of his memory was demonstrated very accidentally. In the living room I had a chess set which John was forbidden to play with. One day, when I was having a long conversation on the telephone in the kitchen, he scattered my chess pieces across the living room floor. When I returned and saw what he had done, I angrily told John to put them back. He immediately put all 32 pieces back exactly where they belonged on the chess board. He was no more than three years old at this time—and still not talking.

When these episodes are all put together, they present a much more optimistic picture than when they actually occurred, as isolated incidents separated by long weeks and months of silence. Eventually, we began to ask doctors why he wasn't talking. At first they said that he would probably talk later, but after more months and then years passed, we began to have him tested for all sorts of things. No one could find anything wrong—and no one had any practical suggestions of what to do. The experts were as baffled as we were.

While John's mother and I were apprehensive about his not talking, there was no sign that John himself was unhappy.

He was master of his own little world. And when we tried to teach him to talk, he showed no real interest.

His mother became more pessimistic than I about John's future. Eventually, she told me that I was just being stubborn in not facing reality.

Since I taught classes at Cornell on Mondays, Wednesdays and Fridays, I could take off all day each Thursday to spend with John and give his mother a day off. He and I usually went to parks or around the campus. One Thursday night, I took him by the office to pick up my mail. As we passed a water fountain, he pointed to it, indicating that he wanted me to pick him up to have a drink.

This seemed to me the time to try to get him to understand that what came out of the fountain was the same thing he saw in lakes and ponds.

"Wah-ee," I said to him, trying to get him to repeat the word and know what this was.

John said nothing but pointed again to the fountain.

"Wah-ee," I said.

John only pointed more insistently at the fountain.

"Wah-ee, John," I said.

He now began to cry in frustration. I immediately picked him up and let him get some water. Then I began to cry.

When John was three years old, his mother decided to take a job. That meant putting John in a nursery school. He didn't like it and what little progress he had made toward talking turned into retrogression. Eventually his vocabulary shrank back to just two words, "rocky" and "wah-ee." He was obviously unhappy and uncertain. Once he loved to have me throw him up in the air and catch him, but now he was apprehensive when I did it, so I stopped. Ironically, his mother's job was unnecessary financially. I had just gotten some consulting work and we had some financial elbow room for the first time. After a few months, however, the project on which my wife was working was finished and John was no longer taken to the nursery school.

John was now three and a half and was still not talking. Nor was there any sign of any way to help him. But help came from a wholly unexpected source. I had to take oral language examinations for my doctorate in economics from the University of Chicago and Professor Earl Hamilton from Chicago was a visiting professor at the State University of New York at Binghamton, not too far away. I could save the airfare to Chicago by driving down to Binghamton and taking the exam there. After I passed my French exams, Professor Hamilton spent some time chatting with me. He asked how things were going in my life in general. I told him that everything was fine—except for my son, who couldn't talk.

"Have you taken him to doctors?" he asked.

"Yes," I said. "All kinds of doctors, all kinds of tests. They can find nothing wrong."

"Is he alert, active?" Professor Hamilton asked. "Does he seem bright?"

"Yes. That's what makes it so puzzling."

"Have you and your wife been able to give him a lot of attention?"

"Not in the past several months. I have been tied up in my work and my wife took a job for a while, so he hasn't been getting the attention he needs. Now I have had some time lately, and I have been trying to teach him to talk, but it just doesn't work."

"Mr. Sowell," he said in a kind and gentle way, "Don't try to teach him to talk—not right now. You just give him lots of love and attention. Take him with you wherever you can. Let him know that you think he is the most wonderful little boy in the whole world. And when he feels confident and secure—he'll talk."

I can't imagine what gave Professor Hamilton this insight, but I was desperate and I followed his advice. For several months, I stopped making any effort whatever to teach John to talk and instead spent far more time with him. He became visibly happier and more secure. Eventually, he indicated that he wanted me to throw him up in the air and catch him again. That was when I thought the time was right to try a little experiment.

I turned on a tape recorder and, as a sort of game, asked John to say "water."

"Wah-ee!" he cried.

When I played it back for him, he was pleased and excited to hear his own voice.

"Rocks, John," I said.

"Rocky!"

I played that back for him too and he was again pleased.

Slowly and in a low-key way, over the next few days and weeks, I began to ask him to say some of the other words he had once used. Each time I played them back for him. It became our little game. Eventually his vocabulary regained its former level—and then continued to grow. All these were single isolated words but, one day when he was watching water going down the drain, I said "down the drain" and he repeated it—his first phrase.

By this time John was just three months away from his

fourth birthday and, now that he had a start toward talking, I thought that he needed a speech therapist to help him develop further. We found a young lady named Miss Duff who was a speech therapist at Ithaca College and who was very good with him. He spoke in whispers but she got him to speak up. From then on, his speech improved in scope and understanding.

Now that he could talk, we discovered that John knew many things. As I drove around Ithaca with him, he would cry out with delight whenever the car went bumping over railroad tracks.

"Railroad tracks!" he cried.

One day I noticed that he was crying out like this before we actually saw the railroad tracks, even when it was a new place that he could not have known from memory. When we returned home I drew a picture and asked John what it was:

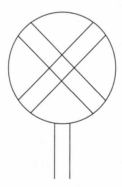

"Railroad tracks," he said. He had figured out that this sign could be seen before we reached the tracks.

Although John was talking and the long nightmare of anxiety was now over, his speech was of course not as advanced as the speech of other children his age, who had been talking for years. Nor did he have experience in verbal interaction with others. In other words, he had a lot of ground to make up.

John's most rapid development came when we drove across the country to Los Angeles, where I was going to teach summer school at U.C.L.A. We took three weeks to get there, stopping along the way. For all that time, John was interacting with his parents all day long as we drove and pointed out things to him. By the time we reached Los Angeles, he could read. He had learned from signs along the highway. His favorite was "No left turn," which he would repeat wherever he saw it. He had turned a corner in his life.

On our way back from Los Angeles at the end of the summer, we stopped and spent the night at the home of friends in Rochester, New York. When I awoke the next morning, I heard the sound of children's songs being played on a piano. It was John—who may never have seen a piano before, but who had learned how to play tunes on his toy xylophone, and immediately realized that the notes were in the same order on the piano keys.

After returning from teaching summer school at U.C.L.A., I immediately had to move again, this time to Brandeis University, where I now had a new appointment. Among the people who came to say goodbye to us before we left Ithaca was a neighbor whom I little knew but who had apparently heard of John. What she said was revealing as to what she had heard from other neighbors. She was the mother of a retarded child and brought us a special toy as a going-away present.

"I understand you have a boy like mine," she said. "So I thought I would bring you this toy that my son likes."

There was nothing to do but to thank her for her kindness—and to be inwardly thankful that I now knew that she was wrong.

————————

The next milestone in John's life was school. By the time he was six, we were back in Los Angeles, where I now had a permanent appointment at U.C.L.A. John did not take well to school, nor did the school take well to him. The teachers I talked with left me very unimpressed and they threw a scare into his mother by telling her that their tests showed John to be "physically uncoordinated." When the tests on which this was based were explained to me, I realized what feeble evidence was being used for such sweeping conclusions.

"Are you aware that this boy can skip rocks across the water with either hand?" I asked. They didn't know and they didn't care. They had their own little test and that was all that mattered to them. In later years, John took up bowling and bowled his first 200 game as a teenager. In December 1996, he bowled a perfect 300 game. "Physically uncoordinated" was one of many labels put on children without any sufficient basis.

By the end of the first semester, I was convinced that John had to be put into a private school. I learned of one that seemed right by accident. One of my U.C.L.A. students brought her young daughter with her to my office and, when I noticed how articulate the little girl was, her mother credited the school she attended. Since I had no other information on private schools, I decided to give this one a try.

It was a school that allowed the children to decide whether or not to go to classes, which was not the way I would have run a school, but perhaps John would be happier there. It turned out that he was. But it also turned out that he never went to math classes. This was puzzling, since he seemed to pick up things concerned with numbers very easily. In any event, I bought him some early math books so that he could learn what he needed at home. He took to them like a duck to water. One night I saw a light on in John's room in the wee hours of the morning and looked in to see how he was. He was working out problems in a third grade math book, even though he was still in the first grade. He was apparently just bored with the math class at school.

Since John's school was not far from U.C.L.A., I would drop him off in the morning on my way to work and his mother would pick him up in the afternoon. In order to give him something to do on the trip, I would show him the mileage on the odometer and ask him to figure out how far we traveled on our way to school and what the number would be when we got there. He soon knew how far the distance was, but he noticed that the number when we got there was sometimes off by a mile. I then had to explain to him that the figure was not exact because we had not counted out to the tenth of a mile after the decimal point on the odometer. This got us into what decimal points meant and soon he had mastered that, so that he now knew the distance to the first decimal point. On the way, he also noticed the freeway signs giving distances in half-miles and quarter-miles, so I explained fractions to him and he quickly learned them.

Over the years, John became something of a math whiz. By the time he was ten, he liked to see if he could add up our restaurant bill in his head faster than the cash register could—and he often won, depending mainly on how fast the cashier was in entering the numbers. When he was 12, after his mother and I were divorced and I had custody of him, we went to Massachusetts, where I was a visiting professor at Amherst College for a semester. It so happened that the head of the math department was my old college roommate. When he had us over for dinner one night, he was surprised at the math problems that John could do in his head.

In one of the little games that John and I played, I would give him three numbers in a series and he was to figure out what the fourth number was and the general formula for the series. For example, I gave him 3, 8, and 23, leaving him to figure out the next number. After thinking for a little while, John said, "The next number is 68—and the formula is $3X - 1$."

My old roommate was astonished—and got out pencil and paper to check this and other things that John did in his head.

Since I was now a single parent, I had to take John with me whenever I traveled. This included a trip to the Educational Testing Service in Princeton, New Jersey, where I gave a talk and stayed overnight. While I was meeting with people at ETS, someone there was kind enough to take John around on a tour and taught him how to use a computer. It was to begin a lifelong fascination with computers for John. After that, he was able to use the computer at Amherst. Later, in his teenage years, after I got him his own computer, he became sufficiently good at programming to get summer jobs at the computer center at Stanford University and at Syntex Corporation. From there, he went on to study computer science in college and made his career in this field.

John became interested in chess by the time he was 12 and began to play in little neighborhood tournaments sponsored by the local public library. From this he moved on to chess tournaments sanctioned by the U.S. Chess Federation. In these various tournaments, there would be small prizes of perhaps ten or twenty dollars, depending on the level of the tournament and where you finished in the standings. One year John won more than a hundred dollars this way. After I acquired custody of him, he and I began to play chess regularly in our apartment at Amherst. At first, I could beat him easily because I had so much more experience, but that did not last very long.

While at Amherst, I drove him down to New Haven for a chess tournament there. A few months later, after we were back in California, and were living in the seaside community of Santa Monica, adjacent to Los Angeles, I drove John down to San Diego for another chess tournament. Fortunately, however, we later discovered another place within walking distance of where we lived, where chess tournaments were held regularly. Sometimes I took part in the tournaments as well. When the U. S. Chess Federation mailed us our official ratings, based on these tournaments, John had the higher rating. It was also becoming clearer, just from our games with each other, that he was now the better player.

We recorded the games we played at home, just as we recorded the official games at the tournaments. Decades later, while going through my files, I came across a game that John and I had played when he was a teenager—and in which he had beaten me in eight moves, without any blunder on my part. For those who follow chess, here are the moves:

JOHN	DAD
1. P–K4	1. P–KB3
2. P–Q4	2. P–Q3
3. N–KB3	3. B–KN5
4. B–QB4	4. P–K4
5. N–B3	5. PxP
6. N–K5	6. BxQ
7. B–B7ch	7. K–K2
8. N–Q5 mate!	

When I set up my chess board to replay this game after all these years, I still could not see after the seventh move how he was going to beat me on the last move. Some days later, when John was visiting me, I showed him the paper on which he had recorded this game. Without setting up the board, he studied the moves on paper, apparently visualizing them in his head. Finally, he said that it was a variation on a famous game played long ago. Chess books were among the few books that he read outside of school during his teen years.

This thumbnail sketch of John's intellectual development necessarily leaves out all sorts of complications that real life always has. Among other things, he was a shy boy who could get very absorbed in what he was doing. These and other characteristics he may well have inherited from me. Once, when I was discussing with an old friend some of John's behavior patterns, he grinned broadly at his wife and said, "Who do *we* know who is like that?" In later years, my sister said that watching John's personal development was like watching history repeating itself.

I too can get very absorbed in what I am thinking about. One day, for example, I was driving through Palo Alto, California, where I lived, and became very preoccupied with some issue that I was thinking about. After I finally resolved the matter in my own mind, and returned to thinking about my driving, I realized that I didn't know where I was or in what direction I was heading—or why. As the blocks went by, I watched for street signs or landmarks that would tell me where I was. Eventually, I recognized the area and realized that I was on Embarcadero, heading east. Now the only question was why, especially since I seldom went to this part of town. Fortunately, I caught a glimpse of an envelope on the seat beside me and suddenly remembered that I was taking it to the post office.

One summer, when John was working at the Stanford computer center, I happened to come out of the Hoover Institution just as he was walking past. We were less than ten feet apart.

"Hi, John," I said, but he walked on, unaware of me. He was obviously absorbed in what he was thinking about, so I only smiled rather than break into his chain of thought.

Somewhere along the way, among all the people I talked with about John's development, I was told that there was a class of boys who had what was called "the three M's"—music, math and memory. Someone else said that John's personal development was like that of the kind of students who end up at places like M.I.T. Once, while waiting in a doctor's office, I encountered another little boy who was not talking and who seemed to me very much like John. His mother seemed so relieved when I told her about my son. About a decade later, a neighbor down the street from me at Stanford had a similar boy who was late in talking—and we lived there long enough to see him grow out of it. Little did I realize that there were many other boys like that—or how little was known about them. That changed only when I wrote the column about John in 1993.

The letters that poured in had many similar stories. One lady said that she burst into tears when she read the column, because her son was also named John, also talked late, and was now in college studying computer science. Many of the parents told stories of anguish, not only over what the future held for their children but also over the readiness of others to label them as retarded, autistic, or whatever—and also over whether they might have done something wrong as parents that might have caused their child to have this problem. However, seldom was there another child in the family who was not talking. This and the fact that nearly all of the children with this pattern were boys suggests that this is an inborn pattern. Further evidence of this came from reading letters from these parents, and in talking to some of them on the phone. I learned that there were often other members of the family with abilities and careers in fields requiring scientific, mathematical or musical ability. My own view is that the parents of late-talking children may have had very little to do with this pattern, except by being the source of their genes.

Although John responded well to great amounts of personal attention, he was not receiving less than the normal amount of attention at the age when children usually begin talking. Apparently neither were the other children I learned of through letters from readers with late-talking children. In fact, some of these children received so much attention that some parents wondered if catering to their child's needs had made him less dependent on developing his own ability to speak. That seems unlikely too, for reasons that will become clearer in Chapter 5.

One case that I learned of independently of responses to the column involved the only pair of parents I know of who were neither panicked nor worried about their child's late talking. Unlike other parents, they did not take him to specialists and did not have him tested for anything. He began to talk at about the same time as the children of parents who did all these other things.

One of the reasons why my research assistant and I were unable to find anything in the literature about this special group of late-talking children with good intelligence may be that there has been little reason for anyone to follow their lives after they began talking. Only their parents are likely to know their stories from beginning to end, and these parents are largely isolated, not knowing anyone else facing the same situation. The child himself typically grows to adulthood unaware of having been a late-talker. John, for example, has no memory of being late in talking and only recalls the red light on the tape recorder I used to get him started.

During the period when our group of parents of late-talking children was forming, I happened to be having computer problems, so that a computer expert was in my home trying to figure out what was wrong, while I was talking on the phone with some of these parents. Later, he mentioned to his mother what he had heard about these unusual children who talk late.

"Like you," his mother said.

two

Children in
the Group

OVER A PERIOD OF THREE YEARS, BEGINNING IN SEPTEMBER 1993, the group of parents of late-talking children grew to 55 families in 24 states, scattered from coast to coast. Because there are two families with two late-talking children each, these 55 families represent 57 children, including my son. Forty-seven of these families share their names and addresses with one another. The other eight families did not make their names and addresses available to the entire group, but only to a limited number of fellow members.

Our group has been very informal, with no dues, schedules, meetings, or rules, except for the unspoken rule of confidentiality concerning what is said within the group. About half the parents have sent out letters to the group as a whole, sharing their experiences and thoughts. A smaller number have contacted other parents by mail or phone, and a few have met in person. Others did none of these things, but most read the letters from other parents and memos from me that circulated within the group. While travelling, I had dinner with two families in Birmingham and another in Virginia. Later, I was able to talk on the phone with one of the late-talking children directly. The others I knew of only from their parents' letters, from questionnaires that were filled in, and from photographs that some parents sent. Reading the letters from the parents was a very moving experience—and one that I can now share with others, with the permission of those concerned.

We can begin with those whose children have already grown out of the late-talking stage.

GROWN-UPS WHO TALKED LATE

John in Missouri

The first letter I received came immediately after my newspaper column about my son was published in May 1993 and before the group was formed, though the mother who sent it allowed her letter to be shared with the group and later circulated another essay on her son's development with the other parents. This lady, whose name is Mary and whose son was also named John, was from Missouri, where the *St. Louis Post-Dispatch* ran my syndicated column under the headline "Put Labels on Cans, Not on Our Children." She wrote: "Amen, and Amen to that!"

"My son, too, acquired a label early in life," she said. He was slow in walking, slow in talking and "drooled so that it looked as if I had poured water on the front of his shirt." Despite the fact that he was "a cheerful child with a bright intelligent look, who followed instructions, my friends and family suggested that in case he should 'get worse' I may have to have him 'put away' one day."

Her son John was past his fourth birthday and still not really talking, but just saying isolated words, when she took him to a doctor. The doctor could find nothing wrong, but suggested that she continue working with her son and if, within six months, he still wasn't talking, "we would think about hospitalizing him to see if there was a reason for his not verbalizing."

"One day I sat on the couch with John to help him color in his coloring book. On the front, H-O-L-I-D-A-Y was spelled and printed in bright colors. He pointed to each one, and repeated the letters after me. He then went back to each letter, and without prompting, pronounced each letter. Although his speech was not 'plain,' he was on his way—at the age of 4 $\frac{1}{2}$."

Even when her son reached school age, the problems were still not over: "After he started school, his teachers complained that he drooled and was I sure that he was normal, his speech was hard to understand."

When her boy was 8 years old, Mary bought an old upright piano from her church so that she could have her daughters learn to play music. After hearing the piano played by Mary's sister, John immediately wanted to play it himself. Since he was a clumsy child, they were reluctant to let him try it and warned him that this was not a toy. Nevertheless, he persisted.

"Play it again, Aunt Bea," he asked. And after she did, he sat down and played the same tune. By the time he was 9 years old, just a year later, John was playing for the 2,000-member congregation of his church, as he continued to do until he grew up and went off to join the Air Force. After his military service, he was torn between becoming a musician and becoming a policeman. Although he had no degree, he taught music in two local schools and gave private lessons, as well as being in charge of music for the city recreation department. Eventually, however, he chose a career in the police department, though he also continued as director of music for his church and continued to give private music lessons. He also writes an occasional column for the local newspaper.

Kevin in Oregon

Carol in Eugene, Oregon, began her letter: "In the past thirty-five years, your article is the first which addressed what we dealt with in our third son."

As a four-year-old child, Kevin "made little attempt to talk, only utilizing about seven simple words or tiny phrases when necessary such as 'wah' for a drink. Pointing was one method for obtaining what he needed while physical gestures or other variations got him what he wanted.

"Folks would ask, 'What's W-R-O-N-G with him?'

"We'd respond, 'Absolutely nothing.' After all, at age four, we'd give him a list of seven to ten directions which he fulfilled immediately. And in order! So how could a little boy be considered stupid or mentally inept when he had more ability to follow directions than that of many adults?"

Still, Carol and her husband were concerned when little Kevin wasn't really talking yet at age 4½. He was also still not completely toilet-trained. "Oh, he no longer peed in his diaper (yes, I said diaper)" but "he still pooped and never cared whether or not he ever got changed. Yuk!"

They sought professional help and it both advanced and retarded his development. The most successful help came from a speech center which was able to expand Kevin's vocabulary rapidly in a few weeks. Still he remained an unusual child in other ways. When he went to preschool at age five, on the first day he sat under a desk the whole time—and the second day he sat on top of a desk the whole time. "From then on, he did fine although he remained independent, preferring to play alone."

At age six, his mother took Kevin to first grade. "At the doorway he refused to enter. I picked him up to carry him in but he put an arm on each side of the doorway, a foot against each lower side of the doorway and there we were! I couldn't get him in. He couldn't get down. I finally smacked his butt. He went in."

"School work and grades came real easy for Kevin. He didn't have to apply himself yet he detested school from that first day until the day he graduated. Kevin literally counted the days until he would graduate." It may be worth noting here that Einstein was put out of school for being a problem. From what we now know about his mental ability, he may well have been bored to death.

While professional help aided Kevin's verbal development, Carol had the misfortune to have a neighbor who was a psychologist who believed in complete permissiveness. "Unfortunately, I was in awe of her," Carol now says, even though the psychologist's own children were brats. Carol backed away from discipline in favor of "reasoning." The net result was that Kevin ran wild.

"Any time things didn't go his way Kevin broke down his entire sleep system, patiently taking off the bedding, mattress, and tearing down the frame. Upon completion of breakdown, he'd put it all back together again. This happened repeatedly for a couple of years." Kevin also learned to take his bedroom door off the hinges and put it back on again. He was about eight years old at the time.

Today Kevin is in his mid-thirties and is a construction contractor.

Carol's daughter also has a son who talked late—in fact, even later than Kevin. When he was 5½ years old, grandson Paul was still saying "mole ho" for mobile home and "pot-cays" for pancakes or hot cakes. But, by the time he was in junior high school, he was on the honor roll.

Colin in Indiana

Annette wrote from a small town in Indiana: "Colin was a late talker. He did not say his name until he was 3 years and 9 months old." She remembers the day because it was her grandparents' 60th wedding anniversary. Before then "he said only a very few single words or sounds. He called his brothers NI and NE and called water LO, and peanut butter LA. The rest of his communication was mostly non-verbal. He would point or try to show us and usually I could figure out what he was trying to communicate."

There was no apparent environmental reason for Colin to be talking late. "He was very loving, happy, brave, and strong willed. He liked working difficult puzzles and had excellent hand-eye coordination. He played weekly at Sunday School and was exposed to a lot of children in other play situations. Because he was our third child, he was included in several play situations with his older brother and their friends. He had a bountiful exposure to many books, toys, games, etc. He was read to often. So we did not understand why Colin wasn't talking, but we could tell he was intelligent and kept hopeful.

"Raised in the same two-parent home, his brothers were also different in their language arts development. Colin's older brother was advanced in his development. He knew the alphabet by the time he was two, began reading fluently in Kindergarten, and tested sixth grade reading level by the time he was in the first grade. He did this because he wanted to; we were not pushing him. He was so curious when he was two that he kept asking what the letters were on the WHEATIES box and it wasn't long until he knew all of his letters. Colin's other brother had the usual language arts development. In the same environment, each of our sons experience very different language arts development."

Colin's hearing was tested and found to be normal. He began working with a speech therapist at a local hospital and, after about six to nine months, his speech became normal. "And once he started talking, he was very talkative, and remains very verbal today. He was by far the most talkative of my three boys while he was growing up and still is today."

As of the time Annette wrote to me, Colin was in his senior year in college. He had already started a little business on the side, using his computer to produce video animations.

Other Adults Who Talked Late

Not all the mothers of children who have now passed through the late-talking stage have written letters for the group. The two who have not are Melanie in a small Florida community and another is Mary in Columbus, Ohio.

Melanie's son was a sophomore in high school when I first heard from her. She wrote to ask for my advice on his selection of a college and, in the course of a subsequent telephone conversation, she just happened to mention that he had talked late. She assumed at one time that he might not develop intellectually as well as his brothers but thought that he would turn out all right. Only after he was old enough to go to school did she realize that he had much ability, when she noticed that he did multiplication problems in his head. He was an honors student in high school.

Mary's son in Ohio had just received his bachelor's degree from the Wharton School when his mother wrote to me. When he went to college, his math score on the Scholastic Aptitude Test was over 700—a level reached by about one percent of those who take the test. The young man in Florida also performed at that level.

Parents whose children have not yet passed through the late-talking stage cannot, of course, be assured of happy endings. But there are some encouraging signs, as well as a few discouraging ones. One of the boys in our group turned out to have severe hearing problems, so his not talking was probably due to his not having heard anyone talking. That was very much the exception, however. A number of the children were labelled autistic, whether by qualified medical professionals or by others such as speech therapists. In at least one case, there has been parental acceptance of the diagnosis, though in other cases there has not been. Twelve of the 37 parents who reported the results of their children's medical evaluations reported that the child was considered autistic, though the most common finding—17 cases—was that no cause was apparent for the child's delayed speech.

The younger children in the group and their parents have often had to cope with something that was apparently not as common when the older children were at the same age— elaborate evaluation sessions by psychologists, psychiatrists, neurologists and other professionals. These sessions, sometimes lasting for hours and conducted in strange surroundings, often proved to be an ordeal for all concerned—the child, the parents and the examiners.

LATE-TALKING CHILDREN

The greatest pressures are on those parents whose children are at the preschool and kindergarten ages and who are not yet talking at a level that would permit them to gain automatic admission to a regular school. Perhaps most important of all, their talking has not yet reached the point where their parents' minds are at ease about their future.

Luke in Arkansas

Luke was born in April 1990 and lives in a small community in Arkansas. He has a younger sister who was speaking in complete sentences before she was two years old. But not Luke.

When Luke was two and a half years old, his parents took him to a speech therapist. There they had an experience that all too many other parents have had: "During my son's first therapy session, the speech therapist asked me if I was ready for a bombshell and then she told me she thought my son was probably autistic. This was very hard on us. Since then we have taken Luke to a developmental doctor, a child psychologist and another speech therapist and they all agreed that Luke showed no signs of autism. This was something my husband and I felt all along, but it was still very reassuring to have it confirmed." As for the first speech therapist, who had recommended having Luke tested by specialists, "her mouth dropped open when she read their report."

Writing in May 1993, right after someone left my column about my son on her husband's desk at work, Luke's mother said: "Luke is talking more than he used to, but still not much more than one syllable (no phrases or sentences yet). Occasionally, he will say two words together, sometimes he says words for a while and then he won't say them for a while.

Other than not talking, there doesn't seem to be anything wrong with him and he is very bright. We know that he has a good memory, he is excellent with puzzles and he has fantastic motor skills. Luke is very loving and affectionate with us and enjoys playing with us and others." At this point Luke was three years old.

Five months later, with Luke now three and a half years old, his mother wrote again, this time to the group that had formed in the meantime: "Luke has always been a very happy child"—active and coordinated, and able to communicate his needs in various non-verbal ways. When he wanted waffles for breakfast, for example, he would pull a stool up to the refrigerator to help him reach up and open the freezer compartment. After removing the frozen waffles from the freezer, he would then open the refrigerator compartment and take out the syrup. After this, he would take the waffles to his parents to heat them up for him—all this without a single word. "Luke does talk," his mother said, "but he limits his sentences to one word, with an occasional two-word sentence."

Luke understood what was said to him when it involved some concrete thing, but abstract concepts like "waiting" did not seem to get through to him—or perhaps he just did not want to wait. "Luke is not very patient when he has his mind set on something. He will often become frustrated and throw himself on the floor in frustration or resistance to us. All this is done without a word, except for crying and an occasional 'no.'"

The youngster's general mental ability, however, seemed fine: "Luke has an excellent memory and does great with puzzles and objects that fit or stack together. Luke shows an interest in toys that open and close, such as trucks with doors or little gadgets with 'compartments' to open and put other stuff inside. Luke loves animated videos or cartoons and will often act out the characters and do his best to sing along."

His mother then described the boy's social behavior: "Luke is responsive to other children who want to play with him, but he likes playing by himself just as much, even when other children are around. Luke will not often recognize or look at new people when he first meets them, especially if anything else has his attention. However, Luke energetically greets us and close friends and relatives when we visit each other. Luke can focus in on certain things that are interesting to him and often ignores any other activity when he is focussed on a favorite toy or video. Luke loves to play outside and entertains himself to a much greater degree than does Hannah."

Like a number of other children in our group, Luke was also late in becoming toilet-trained. His mother described the situation as it existed when he was three and a half: "We are not having much success in potty-training Luke. All of Luke's little friends are potty-trained, yet we still have Luke in 'pull-ups.' We have had some success with #1 and he will go if he only has pull-ups on or just before a shower or bath when he is naked. But, we have had no success at all in getting Luke to go #2 in the toilet. We try to 'catch' him in the process and immediately run to the toilet and set him on it. We have successfully potty-trained Hannah (both #1 and #2) and both of our dogs. But, everything we try doesn't work with Luke."

As far as talking was concerned, Luke was at this point using about 50 words, mostly nouns, though he could also say "crying" and "come on." But he was still having trouble making the sound of the letter L.

In April 1994, right after Luke had turned four, his

mother wrote again. By now, his vocabulary had at least doubled over where it had been about six months earlier and now it included a few phrases like "Where's Daddy?" and "Hey, come back here." He could now pronounce words with the letter L in them, as well as pronouncing words in general more clearly. "Luke routinely says two and three word phrases now, and says hi to people now." He also began to call his parents Mommy and Daddy regularly, "much to our delight."

Social development was also continuing: "He is interacting and playing with other children better as well. Perhaps even more encouraging than the increased vocabulary is this increase in social skills."

Still, his mother was not entirely satisfied, for "we still do not really converse with Luke as we do with Hannah (2½). Luke also tends to favor non-verbal communication over verbal, but at least we are moving in the right direction. Examples of this would be when Luke pulls us to the refrigerator, opens the door and points. We stand there, toe to toe, asking him to tell us what he wants, but he will just point. After a few minutes of this, we will say, 'Do you want a sandwich?' He will say, 'uh, uh,' shaking his head in the no fashion. We will name several other items until it is clear that we have the right item. He will, however, say, 'Thank you,' and so we are thankful for that."

Younger sister Hannah remains more advanced in her talking than Luke is. In fact, "she talks non-stop to him and about him to us. She will tell us Luke did this or Luke did that in front of Luke. I'm hoping Luke will want to defend himself with words of his own. However, right now Luke just deals with Hannah on a more physical level. They play well most of the time, but Luke has a tendency to push, hit or bite Hannah if she is frustrating him. We are working on this and discipline Luke for this, even when Hannah provokes him."

By now, Luke was toilet trained and no longer wearing pull-ups, though he sometimes needed help with his belt or with wiping himself. "Luke did this all on his own; every 'gimmick' we tried when he was younger never worked. We simply had to wait this one out," which meant "no pressure."

In the same letter to the group, Luke's mother said: "We definitely agree with so many of you who have said that the best therapy for our boys (and twin daughters) is to love them, not pressuring them, talking to them, reading to them, but not trying to win every battle (i.e. the refrigerator stand-off). We don't want everything to be a 'no'; we choose our battles carefully, and we win those without exception (with discipline if necessary). But the overall recommendation we have is to let Luke talk at his own pace (like potty training), loving him with attention, play time, touching/kissing/hugging, building him up with each little victory."

Two years later, Luke's mother wrote: "We are very pleased with Luke's progress. Some people who haven't seen Luke in a couple of years say it is truly a miracle. He answers questions now and is doing much better socially. He still will talk too fast sometimes and we can't understand him. It's like he's having to learn to speak a whole different way than the rest of us . . . It's kind of like it's been a foreign language he's had to learn. (Does that make sense?) His sentence order isn't always great and he may use a substitute if he can't come up with the exact word he wants. He is happy, preschool is going great—his teacher said she would bet nobody could pick him out now from the rest of the class just by watching. He even sang on stage for Christmas. (He was perfect—I cried.)"

Andrew in California

Although most of those who wrote to me and to the group were mothers, the father of 3½-year-old Andrew wrote about his development, with a follow-up letter from his mother. "It's about time you all heard from a *dad* of one of our special kids!" he began.

As of 1993, Andrew was "significantly behind the curve for a three-year-old" when it came to talking. He spoke only isolated words, though his mother said that he had "excellence in numbers and music and memory." His parents took him to a whole team of specialists to be evaluated, all these specialists being supplied by the local public school system in a small California community where they live.

"These people were so confused by apparent inconsistencies in his test results that the speech therapist and the psychologist got together" to observe Andrew in his preschool. After seeing him there, they agreed that he could benefit most by individual speech therapy, since his social skills were pretty much adequate for a child his age.

"Andrew started his speech therapy a couple of months ago," his father wrote at the beginning of 1994. "He is doing well, but again the therapist he has been assigned to is bewildered by the mixture of incredible abilities and deficiencies he exhibits. She suggested that Andrew have a medical evaluation to help her design a program for his education. She suggested that he be specifically evaluated for Pervasive Development Disorder, or PDD, which is at one end of the spectrum of conditions known collectively as autism."

It was quite a shock for the parents to be faced with the possibility that something was fundamentally wrong with their child. "From that moment on, every temper tantrum, every phrase repeated over and over in frustration, every grunt uttered in place of English, was a SYMPTOM! Instead of a normal three-year-old testing his limits, we thought of him as a boy with SOMETHING WRONG WITH HIM, someone to be felt sorry for instead of disciplined when he misbehaved. If he had a fit in the grocery store, the looks from other shoppers didn't ask 'What's wrong with him?' They asked, 'What's WRONG WITH HIM?' The dread of his having a lifelong disorder of some sort hung over us like a dark cloud."

When they took Andrew in for his medical examination, the doctor "went absolutely ballistic" at the suggestion that Andrew might suffer from PDD. "How dare they scare you with a thought like that? They're not medical people! What do they know?!" However, the physician passed Andrew on to a psychiatrist, who "basically said, not no, but HELL NO, he doesn't have PDD!"

The weight of the world lifted off their shoulders. "The night we came home from Andrew's evaluation by the child psychiatrist, I tearfully promised him as he slept that I would never let anything interfere with my feelings for him again. No matter what label somebody tries to put on him, one thing will never change—HE'S MY SON!"

Like some other children in our group, Andrew takes readily to music. After he hears his sister play a tune on the piano, he can sit down and play the same tune. He is also very interested in anything numerical—calendars, calculators, digital clocks, and zip codes, for example. He writes equations ($6 + 6 = 12$, $10 + 7 = 17$, etc.) on the backyard fence or on the patio cement. When he writes zip codes, whether real ones or ones that he makes up for fun, he always has the right number of digits and the hyphen in 9-digit codes.

Andrew's reactions to evaluation or therapy sessions have been variable, like that of some other children in the group.

At one session, where the child psychologist talked mostly with his mother, Andrew was fine. This psychologist decided that he was not autistic because he both accepted and initiated physical signs of affection. However, during another evaluation session with a speech therapist, Andrew refused to cooperate, ran around the room, screamed, cried, fell down and kicked the floor.

During a hearing test at age three, he refused to wear the earphones that the examiner gave him. Moreover, when given wooden blocks that were to be used to indicate what he heard, he proceeded to spell out words with the blocks instead. After spelling GENIE with the blocks, he began spelling ALAD—and asked his mother for a D. His mother told him that he was interrupting her discussion with the examiner and the examiner herself said, "You already have the 'D,' Andy." But Andrew knew better. He gave his mother a strange look and then began looking through the blocks for another D, because he knew that there were two D's in Aladdin. The examiner was shocked, though his mother was used to such spelling ability in her three-year-old.

Andrew continues to receive speech therapy "and a lot more discipline than he used to," his father said. "Instead of having everything he does add to our misery, we can now laugh at the cute stuff he does, and love him for everything he is. There's a lot more joy in our house now." Reflecting on the change, his father says: "Has Andrew changed? Of course not. He's the same kid he's always been." The only thing that's different is the way his parents think of him.

The last words in the father's letter offer his advice to the other parents in the group, "lighten up!"

A couple of months later, Andrew's mother wrote to the group:

"An update on Andrew, what a great kid! He is four years old today. I had hoped potty-training would be accomplished by now, but alas, his mom has not yet mastered the training! He goes to preschool three hours a day, three times a week. His teacher is extremely patient and loving. Andrew and I go to speech therapy for one half-hour session, once a week. I hope we can get approval to increase this to two sessions. He regularly uses an 'Andy talk' now, which is not English as we know it. Occasionally a recognizable English word or phrase will sneak in and I can get the gist of what he's thinking. We still rarely *converse*, that is, back and forth communication.

"We do have days when he uses 'standard' speech in short spurts . . . I'd say I get at least one English sentence uttered every day or so now. You may notice since I wrote five months ago, Andrew has begun to use verbs much more! It feels good that we're on an upswing, but for every few steps forward, sometimes there's a step back. When Andy gets sick, all energy goes to that naturally; but then the words disappear and here come the primal sounds again. Same goes if he's tired, frightened, hurt, or excited."

Written communication supplements Andrew's oral communication—and is apparently easier for him. During a tantrum at preschool, complete with screaming and plunging to the ground, the teacher gave him paper and a marker, and he began to write. "She said it helped immediately."

In a postscript, Andrew's mother said: "Andy writes messages all the time to us—but none surprised me more than several weeks ago on the backyard cement. He wrote in chalk, 'Jesus tell me the words.' Thought I was going to faint. I don't know where that thought came from but I guess he wanted to get it out. Writing may be the key to Andy's comfortable outlet. He may grow up to be an author, journalist, ... president! Either way, I'll be so proud (as I am today) to say he's my son!" As regards the reference to Jesus, Andrew's father points out that his son is not some "tortured soul searching for solace," but instead "is a pretty happy little guy." Why he wrote what he did is one of many mysteries about many of the children in our group.

Eric in Alabama

Eric was born in February 1991. He spoke his first word when he was nine or ten months old—but then stopped talking. It was years later before he made a statement using more than one word. In the meantime, this strange retrogression caused his mother to be seriously concerned by the time he was just 13 months old. When she read my column about my son, "I got chills from the similarity to my $2\frac{1}{2}$ year old son."

One doctor diagnosed Eric as having Pervasive Developmental Disorder (PDD), which is to say that he was autistic. "Other doctors just say something is wrong and I needed a label to get my insurance to pay 80% of his treatments." At age $2\frac{1}{2}$, Eric remained speech delayed despite therapy, preschool and "plenty of interaction from the people around him." What was "confusing" to his mother was "Eric's ability to understand and remember things. These most abstract ways of thinking appear to be advanced, yet learning where our ears are can take a week. This is the main reason the doctors continue to have no idea what the problem is."

His mother began "buying every toy or instructional aid that may assist his development." Still his development proceeded at his own pace "while I stayed on edge." She did, however, decide to "'lay off' for a while and relax with Eric and simply enjoy him." Being in our group seemed to help, as she noted similarities and differences between her son and the other children discussed in the letters that circulated within the group.

Eric has had many medical problems, including allergies, ear infections and circles on his tongue. He has been on various medications and has had an operation to remove his tonsils. Writing in 1994, his mother said, "I need to find what keeps Eric sick." A four-hour electro-encephalogram revealed irregular brain activity, perhaps seizures, but the doctor was not sure. Moreover Eric's behavior worsened when he had the circles on his tongue. At one point in 1994, he mother wrote: "After 3 weeks of waking up at 4:30 to give Eric his shot, I couldn't do it any more when I no longer saw an improvement." Sometimes, however, his health would improve dramatically and his mother wondered if people thought she was neurotic because he was so apparently healthy and zestful after having been so terribly sick—vomiting throughout the night—and cranky.

Eric's apparently inconsistent mental development continued. While watching a golfer take a practice swing on television, he exclaimed, "Oh, he missed"—yet he still gave no sign of distinguishing green from blue. On the other hand, like some of the other children in the group, he may simply not have found various questions interesting enough to address them.

At the beginning of 1995, Eric's mother looked back at where they had come in a year. At the beginning of 1994 "I had found no answers, had no support system and saw no improvements in the previous 2 years." Now, she found support in our group and though there were "still no answers," she found that "not all bad compared to some of the answers

I had heard." Nevertheless the quest for some answers took her and her son to new cities, new specialists and more medical tests. One doctor in New Orleans spent two hours with them.

"He basically said I was right, something was not the norm with Eric and he was an odd child. He asked me if I had ever read anything on Einstein and that Eric may fall into a group of highly intelligent children. He said studies had been done but not extensive ones because, once the children are okey, parents stop seeking doctors and no one ever knows what happens to the child." He advised her to do nothing for the next six months and to run some hormone tests if his growth had not taken a spurt by then.

A preschool for which she had high hopes "proved to be a flop." It was chaotic and the children were not paid much attention. Eric disliked the school "and most days I left almost in tears." She found another preschool for Eric "and he made major improvement almost instantly.

"His speech picked up, he began singing songs, his play is developing, his imagination is growing ... The first day I picked him up I asked him if he liked school (as I always did but got no answer, assuming he didn't understand my question) and he said, 'Yeah mama!' I guess in his way he was letting me know that the other school was not for him. Since that first day, he has steadily gone uphill. I haven't had any of the bizarre behavior like I did the months in the other school."

His speech—or at least vocalizing—also improved. "Eric is talking all the time now (of course only a select few can understand him). But the doctors say if he continues this growth in the next 6 months he may be okay. Of course they strongly suggested speech therapy, but I am waiting on that. I know he is not near a 4 year old, which he will be in February, but I want to give him time on his own."

Medical problems continued, necessitating emergency room treatment several times. At various times, different doctors said conflicting things. Moreover, as the wife of a military pilot, Eric's mother often had to face domestic problems alone—or rather, with her mother.

One day, someone in a health food store strongly urged her to get Eric off the prepared juice drink he was addicted to. Fearing a fit from Eric if she changed, she nevertheless ventured to offer him plain orange juice. "Over the next several days I noticed a dramatic change in his personality and he was actually trying to communicate with language." Her skeptical parents, however continued to give him the prepared juice drink "and he went wild on them." His mother decided that there might be something to diet after all, despite some doctors who had pooh-poohed the idea.

"Over the last month Eric has turned into someone totally different." He "is talking continuously," adding words to his vocabulary every day. He not only understood what was said to him, "I can reason with him" and he "sleeps like a rock."

"The best thing is he is interacting with people and the world around him. He always played well but only to himself. He is beginning to play games like "'got your nose' and wanting us to sing songs to him. When I read to him now, he's not just sitting there; he listens and talks to me about what is happening and what will happen. He no longer watches TV silently, he is constantly telling me what is on the screen."

His shots, however, continued—and on days when he didn't get them, his behavior retrogressed so badly that "his preschool teacher knows the second I drop him off." Dosages have had to be adjusted and there was the possibility of having to add more medication, though his mother was reluctant to do so.

As of 1996, Eric was in kindergarten—and was happy. "Eric adores his teacher, which is most of the battle for him. I also think she enjoys his sense of humor. You can imagine how important this is."

Twins in Alabama

The first girls in our group were twin girls in a small town in Alabama. Their parents' experience, however, was very much like that of the parents of late-talking boys. For years "family, friends, day care workers, and a number of so-called 'experts' attempted to label our daughters as autistic, or having pervasive development disorder (PDD). Their never-ending efforts to assist us in moving through the 'denial phase' of the grief process were more than we could bear at times."

The twins, Amy and Laura, were 7 years old when their parents joined the group. By then they were talking, but not at a level achieved by other children their age who had been talking longer.

According to their parents, "They use language to communicate their needs, to ask about things in the environment, and to comment about what they see. They do not seem to be bothered in the least by their inability to communicate at the more advanced level of most 7 year olds." However, they "regularly use 4–6 word sentences and occasionally a sentence with as many as 8 or 9 words." They first began to engage in back-and-forth conversation when they were four years old. By the time they were 7, their vocabulary was "close to normal for their age."

As babies, the twins sat up, walked and talked at the usual ages. When they were 6 weeks old, they were left with a baby-sitter so that their mother could return to work, and a few months later they were left in a day care facility. The day care director was the first of many people to express concerns over the girls' mental development. They did not interact socially with the other children or with the teacher, walked on their toes, spent much time gazing at their hands, and beat their backs against the wall—all characteristics of autistic children. On the other hand, by the time they were $2\frac{1}{2}$ years old, they could recite the alphabet as well as identify the letters in random order, and could identify numbers up to 20, as well as identifying common items in the environment.

The girls' pediatrician was not as concerned as the day care director, who thought they might be autistic. The pediatrician "said that Amy and Laura's development was not all that unusual for twins, and that many 'normal' children did a lot of the things they were doing. She thought they would begin to use the language more socially when they got ready, and that they would probably outgrow the other unusual behaviors. She also told us that she saw many 'abnormal' children sent to her from day care workers and teachers who could not accept the fact that children develop at their own rates. In essence, she told us to be patient and give them a chance to grow up, and that they were *not* autistic."

Despite this medical opinion, the twins' teacher and grandmother "were convinced that the pediatrician didn't know what she was talking about" and that the parents were "in a state of denial." Under pressure, the parents then took Amy and Laura to a neurologist. "He agreed wholeheartedly with the pediatrician, and said that he didn't see anything severe enough to justify placing the 'autism' label on them."

He too felt that they would mature when they got ready. "He indicated that with autism the symptoms (back-beating, toe-walking, hand-gazing, etc.) tended to get worse, not better. His general feeling was that the twinship was largely responsible for some, if not all, of the delays. He also said that he thought their use of language would increase in 8 or 9 months."

Like some of the boys in our group, the twin girls were also late in being toilet-trained. As three-year-olds, they "simply were not interested in being big girls" and neither candy nor other rewards led them to use the toilet consistently, even though they were wearing training pants and had many individual "successes" in using the toilet. "What happened was that *we* had become toilet trained. They relied upon us to know when it was time to go, and to take them in time to avoid an accident."

When the girls were enrolled in a kindergarten class for 4-year olds, they were the youngest children among the 14 in their class. Although their teacher said that they were "the smartest in the class," their "hard-headedness and immaturity made them a real handful when the task at hand involved something in which they were not interested." Their problems included not staying in their seats, getting into things after being told not to, bothering other children's crayons, taking other children's food at lunchtime, not staying on their mats at nap time, and of course not being toilet-trained. The parents were asked to take them out of the kindergarten.

After the twins were removed from kindergarten and kept at home, they made remarkable progress. "A few weeks after they were home with us, we were shocked when Amy, at the age of 4½ suddenly began to utter a number of 3–5 word phrases." While out strolling in the neighborhood with the girls, their mother paused at a street sign and was surprised when Amy said, "Come on, let's go." As they resumed strolling, she added, "walking in the street." A couple of months later, Laura also began using the language to express herself. Their mother says, "I am still amazed at how accurately the pediatric neurologist had predicted when they would begin using the language." But they were not out of the woods by any means.

As Amy and Laura were approaching their fifth birthday, they were taken for an evaluation by a team of various experts—none with a medical background and all affiliated with the school system—to determine where they should be placed in the upcoming school term. The team's diagnosis was "moderate to severe autism" and the parents were urged to put the girls in the state's autism school. Unwilling to accept this diagnosis, the parents went to a center for development and learning disorders where "a four hour whirlwind evaluation with a variety of 'experts'" produced a similar diagnosis of pervasive developmental disorder (PDD) and a similar conclusion was reached that the twins be placed in the state's autism school. The parents resisted this and instead placed them in a class for early childhood education for the handicapped in a nearby school.

"After two and a half years in this class, we feel that they have made remarkable progress." Near the end of their first year there, the girls became toilet-trained—after the parents stopped taking them to the bathroom. Left on their own now, the girls became completely toilet-trained after a few accidents. "Academically, they have mastered almost all of the content covered in a regular kindergarten curriculum. They have also learned that they must behave and conform to expectations at school. With proper placement next year, and

I'm not sure yet what that will be, they will hopefully catch up with their peers within the next few years."

That was where things stood in the spring of 1994, when the children were still in "a special education class for children with minor learning disabilities," where they received individual speech therapy 4 days a week. But now more decisions loomed on the horizon: "In the fall they will have to be placed in another class because of their age. We are *not* looking forward to another battle with the school system authorities, who are still fixated on the 'autism/PDD' labels." Fortunately, when the fall came, other classes became known to the parents and the girls were enrolled in two separate classes. Their behavior improved in the new setting and an enormous weight was lifted off their parents' shoulders. However, this was not due to good placement by the school authorities. The first school the girls were sent to had a "know-it-all military style teacher with a Mickey Mouse curriculum," their mother said, but she removed them back to the first school, where they did fine. "The lesson we learned from this nightmare was that you *cannot* trust the school authorities to assess your child and decide what's best for him."

Their mother's progress report on the twins at the end of 1994 indicated uneven levels of development but continuing advance across the board, including "the areas of language development and social skills." By this time, they were able to talk in six- to eight-word sentences, and occasionally longer ones. More significantly, they initiated more conversations and the back-and-forth discussions continued longer than before. Still, their improved speech had not completely closed the gap between their performance and the norms for their age. Pronouns and very general questions were still a problem for them and their reading lagged a year or so behind their age level. Meanwhile their mastery of computers, videocassette recorders and other electronic equipment was outstanding. "Perhaps one day they'll choose to study computer science or engineering!" their mother said.

As a layman who has seen these children only once, in the artificial setting of a hotel dining room while I was travelling in their vicinity, and who knows only what their parents have told me, I am nevertheless struck by how many of their problems are serious primarily because they occur in an institutional setting, where conformity to an organized routine is necessary to some extent—and is often imposed far beyond that extent.

As the school year neared an end in the spring of 1994, the class that Amy and Laura were in was also approaching its dissolution, as the children in it reached the age at which they must move on to some different placement. A placement conference again put the school officials in conflict with the parents, but the situation seemed to be resolving over the summer when they learned of a special class with a teacher who seemed to have some of the academic goals of the parents. However, the placement never became official, despite repeated assurances. As the summer wore on with no decision, the official in charge stopped returning the parents' phone calls, though the secretary called back to say that everything was on track. Only very close to time for school to begin did they learn that the promised class had been cancelled. As late as the Friday before school was to start the following Monday, the parents still did not know where their children would go to school.

At this juncture, they heard of a highly-touted teacher, recommended by both school officials and by mothers of children who had had her. Although she taught 17 miles away, the twins were enrolled in her class. Within a week, the parents noted improvements in the girls' behavior. However, there was a high price to pay for this improvement: The twins had to catch the school bus before 7 A.M., in order to arrive at 8:30, and they had to leave school at 2:30 P.M. in order to get back home by 4:00. Not only did they spend 3 hours a day on busses, transferring en route, they also missed an hour of school a day, in order to make bus connections. Moreover, the highly-touted teacher was not focussing on academic work, so that what the girls were receiving was "deluxe baby-sitting," according to their mother. Their father began to drive the twins to school in the morning, in order to cut the time in transit, but he let them ride back on the busses, which they enjoyed.

Soon even the good behavioral benefits of the new school began to disappear, as Laura complained that the teacher pulled her hair and struck her with a board. Their parents yanked them out of school in early November, keeping them home for 3 weeks while they tried to think of an alternative, despite threats of legal action being taken against them for failing to have their daughters in school. In December, after more discussions with school officials, the parents reluctantly agreed to another placement in which the twins would be separated for the first time.

Over the next academic year, the struggles of the parents with the public school system continued—the parents wanting the girls to be given more academic work, while the school resisted. Although the educators were shown more advanced work which the girls did at home, the school remained unwilling or unable to move much in that direction. One reason was the variety of other children with other special needs in the classes to which the twins were assigned. The enormous amounts of time required by some of these other children with serious disabilities left the teachers juggling their time between providing a little academic work for the twins, when other demands on their time permitted, and letting them watch entertainment videos when the time was not available to give them academic work.

Throughout their schooling, the girls' misbehaving has made a placement in regular classes impossible. Their lagging speech development has also complicated the situation, though their speech has approached normal in quality, even if not in quantity, and their vocabulary is good for their ages. Because of their years in special classes, where academic work has been neglected, largely because the other children in such classes for other reasons are unable to do very much, the twins are academically behind where other children their age are. They would, however, be even further behind were it not for the amount of academic work their parents give them at home.

By far the best educational experience for the twins began in the fall of 1996, when they were placed in a regular third-grade class with assistance, where they did work comparable to the other third graders and where their behavior improved and they began to have friends and develop socially. Although two years behind where they would have been in a normal academic situation, the girls' progress has heartened their parents and led to the hope that they can gradually reach the point where they can go into regular classes.

Perhaps some day these girls will appreciate what fortitude it took for their parents to fight to protect them from the system. Not all parents have this fortitude, as the mother herself noted. She said: "The real sadness, though, is that many parents don't even bother to get informed and stand up for what is best for their children. I understand that many parents in our school district do not even attend placement meetings or meetings with their children's classroom teachers, speech therapists, etc. They simply sign the necessary forms and the school system takes it from there!"

David in Texas

A younger child named David has not yet reached that stage. He was tested by a school district at age 3½. His parents wrote that "a 'team of experts' asked us tons of questions and observed David. . . . He cried and screamed and kicked when they tried to get him to perform activities. The psychologist liked the fact that David was so curious about things. But when David put the stacking rings in the same order that he found them (which was wrong) this concerned the psychologist enough that he remarked on it a few times. David put his alphabet in order separating upper and lower case letters appropriately, worked puzzles, etc. The psychologist said he had many skills. Well after an hour and fifteen minutes of this the team asked us if we could come back two weeks later to have him specifically evaluated for autism."

At the second meeting, "the autism team evaluated him. They started off blowing bubbles for him which he loved. He smiled, laughed, popped bubbles, made a lot of eye contact," but things "went downhill" when they stopped the bubble play and brought out the puzzles. When the child fussed at having his fun stopped, this supposedly "showed resistance to change"—one of the characteristics of autistic children (as well as millions of other children and adults). "They put puzzle after puzzle in front of him. As soon as he completed one they took it away—which caused more fussing—and put another one in its place. He worked the puzzles quickly, they were timing him, and worked puzzles for 7 year olds. They were very impressed with his puzzle skills but were also impressed with the fact that he fussed when they took a puzzle away as soon as he worked it. He is only 3½, I think I would have fussed too." Yet this typically childish behavior was read as having such deep significance that it led to a diagnosis of "slight to moderate autism." The team "said his IQ was normal for his age. His high IQ behaviors like puzzles, etc. average out with the low IQ language to make a normal IQ." This mechanistic averaging may tell us more about the testers than about the child.

David's parents then consulted a private professional in the field who "said not to let the autism label scare us" because "it is a label that is used a lot for funding reasons." Public schools get more money from the government for children who have been put in some abnormal category, so self-interest is another reason for their being prone to put labels on children. Research is still another reason for labels. The autism team referred to David as a "gold mine" and were anxious to follow his development. That such a team could call a child a "gold mine"—that is, see him in terms of how he could help them, rather than vice versa—is yet another indication of the mine fields that parents of late-talking children must walk through.

Like some of the other children in our group, David has had sudden dramatic improvements in maturity. A mother who helps in his preschool occasionally remarked on how much he had improved in the month since she had seen him last. When she opened his box of raisins for him at lunchtime, he said, "Raisins! I like raisins!" My son's speech was not that advanced at that age. But, fortunately, he was not evaluated by some school team concerned about "funding" or looking on him as a "gold mine" for their research.

Billy in California

Billy was a large baby at birth—eight pounds exactly—and his development was on schedule or a little ahead of schedule on everything except talking. He crawled at 6 months, was standing a week later, and walked before he was 11 months old. He learned to ride a tricycle at 18 months and could use a videotape cassette recorder and a computer when he was two and a half years old. At that time, however, his parents became concerned because he was still not talking. Moreover, his preschool teacher was also concerned that he did not seem to understand what she was saying to him, in addition to his not talking, and his frustrated behavior likewise lent some urgency to a need to deal with his inability to speak.

Billy was tested by a pediatrician, an audiologist, a speech pathologist, and a developmental psychologist, all at age two and a half. The parents were jolted by the psychologist's diagnosis of "pervasive developmental disorder," since this meant autism. However, the appropriateness of the word "pervasive" seemed especially questionable, in view of all the other ways in which Billy was advanced in his development, including being able to do puzzles at a four-year-old level. A second opinion by a speech pathologist went counter to the diagnosis of "pervasive developmental disorder."

"It took months for us to sort through all the conflicting opinions and contradicting treatments suggested by the many professionals that we have consulted," his mother said. "Through trial and error and trusting our parental instincts, we have learned to work with our son, and he has made astounding progress. Unfortunately, even with this progress, he does not test well." Like a number of children in our group, and like my son, Billy did not automatically perform on cue, even when asked to do something that he had already done on other occasions.

Billy's memory has been "astounding," according to his mother: "He can tell you which parent attended which field trips during the past year and does not leave out a single field trip." Before he was four years old, Billy knew which of his computer games were in Windows and which were in DOS, and could find his way to either without help. Still, because of his late talking and the conflicting evaluations, doubts lingered. "I am interested in discovering what I might expect in the future," his mother wrote at this point. "Of course, none of the professionals will offer any kind of prognosis." The Autism Research Institute was contacted for an evaluation by questionnaire through the mail. The resulting evaluation did not indicate autism. Still, when he was seen by a school pathologist, she concluded that he needed further evaluation, in part because he refused to answer any questions.

"Due to the conflicting messages we have been receiving," his mother said, "we are left to trust to our own instincts. It is hard to do that, when you are not a trained professional and the professionals tell you that you are in denial!"

Like many of the children in our group, Billy has been very strong-willed. During his "terrible twos" his tantrums "could last for hours." However, he could also be very affectionate. "He loves to be held and cuddled. He craves attention and likes to be involved with whatever others are doing." While he liked to rough-house, he had also developed the habit of saying things like "excuse me," "please," and "thank you." By this time, just before turning four, Billy was speaking in five- to seven-word sentences.

Three months after Billy turned four, his mother wrote again about his improvement: "He is better able to deal with disappointment and doesn't have the tantrums he used to have." The persistence that once expressed itself in tantrums "has enabled him to learn things like putting together puzzles. He can stay with the task for a long period of time with no frustration. For example, if he tries a wrong piece, he'll just say 'oops, try again' and look for another piece."

When continuing dissatisfaction with the evaluations of Billy led his parents to seek a second opinion, no one would give one "without a referral from our pediatrician or reading the report from the psychologist." So they passed on getting a second opinion that would be more like a first and a half opinion. Finally, however, they found another speech therapist. Her opinion was that he did *not* need the sort of therapy recommended by others, and said that the clinic he had been to was notorious for "over-diagnosing" some children.

The mixed signals from professionals was paralleled by mixed signals from relatives. Some relatives said that there was nothing wrong with Billy but others said that he "cries a lot." His mother did not think that he cried a lot, except around some of the relatives who came in large family gatherings. "He was overwhelmed with the noise and people he hardly knew coming into his face and saying 'How are you Billy?'" However, he was all right with those relatives whom he saw on a regular basis. "He would go to their house, give them hugs or tickles and run off to play with his cousins. He would give his uncles and grandpa 'high-fives' and his grandma kisses."

Nevertheless, Billy's parents joined a support group run by the psychologist who had diagnosed Billy as having pervasive developmental disorder. The more they heard about the other children, the more convinced they became that Billy was unlike the autistic children of other parents in the group. Months later, at a picnic, one of these parents pulled his mother aside and said: "I've been watching Billy all day looking for signs, and I could not see *one*—he seems so normal!"

Still, the parents were not yet prepared to completely reject professional advice. In fact, his mother said in retrospect, they themselves put Billy's behavior under a microscope, worrying about things that other parents simply saw as cute when their children did them. They signed up for group and individual therapy at the same clinic where he had been evaluated. "The first group they put him in was with 4 autistic kids. We'd watch him through the observation window and get sick to our stomach that they were lumping him into that group. We told his therapist that we thought it was the wrong group for him and she said give it a chance. It was obvious that she believed in the psychologist's diagnosis." However, Billy's preschool teacher was allowed to come and observe also. "After just one minute, his teacher exclaimed, 'TAKE HIM OUT OF HERE! THEY ARE GOING TO UNDO ALL OF THE PROGRESS WE HAVE MADE WITH HIM! THIS IS NOT BILLY!'" Now Billy's mother grew angry that the therapists had not seen the same thing, but were relying on the psychologist's report, rather than on what was happening in front of their own eyes.

Still the parents sought other professional opinions—and they continued to get conflicting advice. Although a computer was proving helpful to Billy in learning language, both at home and at school, the therapist declared that a computer had no place in a child's curriculum until at least junior high school. One of the good things to come out of these continued attempts to get some answers from professionals, however, was that a well-known specialist on autistic children declared that Billy definitely did *not* have "pervasive developmental disorder."

Billy himself was apparently growing more hostile towards the therapy and testing sessions, as well as the speech sessions. "We would actually observe him tightening his mouth as he approached the building where the sessions were held." Moreover, his teachers said that Billy did better at school on days when he did not have speech therapy. His therapist complained, "I can't adequately assess him because he just isn't able to cooperate with the standardized testing." The issue, however, may not have been what he was *able* to do but what he was *willing* to do. The therapist herself "said that whenever she pulled out books, he would look at them just fine. But when she pulled out her 'testing' book, he'd tell her angrily: 'Put it away!'"

As for his general behavior at age four, his parents felt that he had come a long way. "Now that he has language he can be reasoned with. For example, we were in the hardware store this weekend and he wanted to climb the ladder. I told him 'no' and sensed that a power struggle was about to break out. He said, once again, 'I go up there.' Luckily I thought about it (rather than reacting) and said to him, 'You don't work here!! You have to work here to go up the ladder!' He laughed and said 'Ma ma work here?' I said, 'No, Mama doesn't work here—I can't go up the ladder!' and he laughed. This would have been a long, drawn out tantrum a year ago!"

In assessing Billy's overall behavior at age four, his mother regarded his behavior problems as "typical of a child his age—maybe amplified by the frustration and lack of adequate communication skills." Moreover, on "the flip side of all this," he had certain good behavioral traits that many other children his age lack: "He waits his turn in line. He never grabs a toy another kid is playing with. He doesn't hit, kick, bite, etc." In fact, she has had to teach him to stand up for himself when other children try to take his toys from him or push him around.

In school, Billy became attached to a little girl named Heidi "and the teachers said they were inseparable!" He talked incessantly about her at home. Unfortunately, Heidi's parents separated and she began to go back and forth between her father and mother every two months. The teachers worried about how Billy would react to her absence. But he would now play by himself or briefly with other kids. When his mother asked him if he missed Heidi, he replied: "I miss Heidi, I play with Alex now." When Heidi came back, she and Billy were now in different classes. However, he ran over to her on the playground and said to the other kids: "*My* Heidi."

"As for now, my husband and I think Billy is doing *Wonderful!* We count our blessing every day about all of his progress." His teacher notes that he is still "different" but his parents have stopped all the special services. His teacher continues to complain about his behavior and misbehavior, much of it in terms that conflict with what his mother observes at home. How much of his school behavior is bad in itself and how much is due to the needlessly narrow norms of the school are unanswerable questions. However, one symptom of such norms was his teacher's reaction to an episode on the playground: "She said that since his friend Heidi came back, they've been observed laughing and chasing each other. They were doing something where they were both putting buckets on their heads and laughing about it. But, the teacher noted, they were 'not interacting.'"

With other children, Billy seemed to have difficulties in handling social relations and tended to withdraw into some favorite solitary activities, such as doing puzzles. One "resource teacher" who observed him "said that Billy would come in from the playground and go straight to the puzzle to 'zone out' and gear up for the group. After the puzzle was done, he seemed 'ready' to try the interaction. He gave off signs all over the place that he wanted very badly to fit in and play with the other kids, but didn't quite know how. He would approach kids involved in an activity and stand there and stare, waiting for something to happen. Apparently, he appeared very tense at these times."

After hearing this, the parents had conferences with the director of the center and with Billy's regular teacher. Once his teacher was advised of the situation, she began to prompt him about how to behave in social encounters that were awkward for him. For example, when she found him obviously wanting to join some activity, she would say to him, "Billy, do you want to play too?" When he nodded to indicate that he did, she would then say, "Say, 'can I play too?'" It worked. "After just two days," his mother said, "she's successfully drawn him away from zoning out on the puzzles and has involved him in group activities. It's amazing what a little effort can accomplish!"

While Billy's improvements were welcome, public school policies were such that he was not badly off enough to qualify for an aide to help him over the rough spots socially, which occur more often when there are large numbers of children around. If Billy were to be labelled autistic or as having "pervasive developmental disorder," that would improve his chances of getting help. His mother, however, has resisted that label, even though she was told that "professionals don't see the harm in using a label to get services," that it is "just a matter of paperwork to them." But labels can influence how teachers and others treat a child, as had already happened. Billy's parents engaged a graduate student who had been recommended by his therapist. This student began to visit him at school once a week for an hour, to help him and his teachers learn to cope with social situations that have been going badly.

After several months, Billy's mother wrote to the group that the graduate student "made a world of difference," not only in extricating Billy from various situations but also in educating his teachers, who often misunderstood what was happening and why. The graduate student also said that Billy was not particularly more restless or mischievous than other boys during "circle time" and "felt that he might participate more if circle time were more interactive and less 'sit and listen.' The teachers did a lot of singing and the songs were above Billy's level of expressive language. He often sat and listened to the songs instead of singing. While this did not bother me, it seemed to bother the teachers quite a lot." In short, the rigidities of the routine and the lack of comprehension of the teachers were creating problems at school that Billy did not have at home.

Apparently what the graduate student had that the teachers did not always have was common sense and a willingness—and the time—to try to understand a particular child's problem. Billy's biggest problems came out on the playground, where he did not have the skills to negotiate through social encounters. For example, if the graduate student noticed that Billy had his eye on a shovel that another child was using, she would ask him, "Do you want that shovel?" When he nodded, she would then prompt him, "Go ask the

child, 'Can I have that shovel please?'" If he was not successful, the graduate student would say, "Ask him, 'Can I have it
when you're done?'" Once Billy discovered that using
phrases like these in various situations usually got better
results than crying, he began to use them on his own. The
graduate student also explained to Billy the unspoken social
rules of the playground and of life, things that some teachers
regard as a nuisance to do. One assistant teacher even
accosted Billy's mother in the hallway to complain that the
graduate student was not doing anything and that what Billy
needed was a full-time, one-on-one aide—or a mother who
stayed home with him.

This confrontation led to conferences, a sort of armed
truce with the assistant teacher, and suggestions for further
evaluation. Although the school district might have supplied
the evaluation, by now his mother was sufficiently skeptical to
pay for an outside evaluation. Among other things, she and
the outside professionals "discussed ways to teach the teachers
to be more interactive during circle time and address him at
his level of understanding. I volunteered to buy a 'circle time
kit' that I saw at a teacher supply store. It contained props for
interactive circle time activities . . . The primary teacher was
thankful for the gift and it was a nice way to promote more
interactive activities without offending the teachers."

It might be noted here that any number of people have
commented in general, over the years, on the fact that teachers seem to want little boys to sit quietly far more often than
little boys are likely to do. That none of this had filtered
down to the teachers, or made a dent in their practices, may
say something about the caliber of the people involved or
their capacity for thinking beyond the routines and fetishes of
the system.

Problems of a very different sort suddenly loomed on the horizon for Billy. He began to close one eye, sometimes the left and sometimes the right. At first, it was thought that he was playing some kind of game. But his mother began to worry when the periods when he did this grew longer and longer, until he would keep one eye shut all day long. When she asked his pediatrician for a referral to a pediatric ophthalmologist, the pediatrician declared, with an air of certainty, "it doesn't sound like his eyesight. If it were, he'd be squinting. It sounds like a facial tic to me." He then suggested waiting a few weeks to see if it went away.

"I cannot even describe how angry I felt at this remark," Billy's mother said. "I told the pediatrician that if Billy had not been given a label, he would not hesitate in recommending an eye exam. He finally gave me the name of a pediatric ophthalmologist who has 'worked with kids like Billy' and I made the appointment right away."

Despite the pediatrician's dogmatism, the examination showed that Billy did in fact have a serious eye problem, leading to double vision—and to the danger of blindness in one eye if it were not corrected. Fortunately, it could be corrected with glasses and was. Among other things, the ophthalmologist said that he sees children with "pervasive developmental disorder" frequently and that Billy behaved like none of them. "He also said that he frequently has parents report that their child's behavior, cooperation, learning and overall disposition had improved once their vision was corrected." This was in fact how it turned out in Billy's case. When he put on his new glasses, he "loved them right from the start . . . When he walked into his bedroom after putting them on, he just stood there, staring at all of his toys, looking around at everything. He wanted to play with all of them at once! The teachers reported a similar situation at school the next day. They said that he looked at everything and everyone as though seeing them for the first time. After about a week, the teachers commented that they were astounded at how differently Billy behaved. He seemed less stressed on the playground. He did not move away when the other children got close to him. He seemed less distracted and more attentive during circle time."

Although still being pressed to put Billy into one of the various programs for children with special problems, his parents resisted and continued to use the graduate student. Eventually, however, the graduate student became pregnant and was unsure whether she would come back after having her baby. "She had planned on helping me find a replacement. Instead, she called me one night and suggested that we were wasting our money because Billy no longer needed her help. We agreed that she would work up until Thanksgiving. It was really hard to give her up. Her notes were very comforting to us. They provided valuable insight into his day. Now I would have to be like the 'other moms' and rely on Billy to tell me about his day. At least he was beginning to do that!"

In the summer of 1996 Billy's mother reported continued progress on several fronts and that he now plays the piano. By this time, he was so advanced on the computer that he was able to help his mother do some things in Windows 95 and he has likewise helped the teacher use the computer at school. Socially, family members have commented that "he is a changed kid from last year. He has made a couple of new friends, answers the telephone and came in first in his kindergarten in making free throws in basketball, making eight out of eight, compared to three out of eight for the runner-up. In his piano class he "has been known to show off by playing songs with his eyes closed, to impress the teacher."

Joshua in Arizona

Joshua was born in March 1990 and lives in a small community in Arizona. He was not the first member of his family to talk late. His uncle did not talk until he was 4 and, during that time, the uncle's younger sister had to interpret what he said to others —as is also the case with at least one of the boys in our group. A cousin also talked late.

Because of this family history, Joshua's mother was not too worried that he was still not talking when he turned two. She described him as a "happy-go-lucky" child—until he was about $2\frac{1}{2}$ to 3 years old. Now when things did not go his way, "he let out a scream that would put hairs on your chest," she said. When he did this in public, the mother said, "I wanted the earth to open up and swallow me." All it took to set him off was her taking something away from him, or his dropping his toys, or just his mother's saying "no" to him, even in a nice way.

Joshua "seemed oblivious of dangerous settings, such as busy streets" and had to be held by the hand whenever he went out. On the other hand, when his parents wanted him to walk, he would often cling to their legs until he was picked up. The net result of these embarrassing difficulties in public, *"we led very sheltered lives."* As the youngest child, used to the attention of a full-time mother, Joshua could not be left with a baby-sitter unless he was already fast asleep.

Joshua loved watching "Sesame Street" on television but had no interest in talking. "I tried teaching him words," he mother said, "but he had *no desire* to repeat anything. He would ignore me, get angry, never even *tried*." When he needed to communicate, he would grunt, point to what he wanted or knock on the refrigerator when he wanted something inside it.

Like some of the other children in our group, Joshua was delayed in toilet training. He learned to urinate in his potty chair at 2½ years of age, but not to have bowel movements there in any predictable way. He usually held off until it was almost too late. "We had to pick him up, run like heck," and hope to get to the toilet on time. Then, one day, he just started going on his own.

By his third birthday, Joshua spoke only a few words like "Ernie" and "Bert" for the Sesame Street characters, but he said these few words very seldom. Moreover, he did not like to play with other children and still screamed when he dropped his toys. Moreover, unlike other children in the group, Joshua did not seem to understand directions. "'Go get that ball' might as well have been 'explain the theory of relativity,'" his mother said. She began to worry about all the things that might have made him the way he was—the long labor she went through when he was born, hearing problems, tongue problems, or the fact that his parents met his needs without his having to talk.

One day, sitting in a hospital waiting room, "we discovered that Joshua knew all the numbers, all the letters in the alphabet and counted to 20 when he read them from a blackboard in the room." His parents were stunned because they had not taught him any of that. As with toilet training, he just did it on his own when he was ready.

When Joshua was 3 years and 7 months old, his parents decided to take him to a class they had heard about for children with delayed learning or handicaps. "That was an experience," his mother said. "Joshua did not cooperate at all. He went around trashing the room. Had one of the worst days he ever had. He wouldn't sit down, wouldn't answer questions I *knew* he could." The school people couldn't even screen him to determine if he could attend. "What he needed was a spanking," his mother said, "but he knew I didn't do it in public."

Apparently this experience was traumatic for Joshua as well as for his mother. His development went backward afterwards and he began soiling his pants again, after having been toilet-trained. He also started waking up in the middle of the night and crying until his mother lay down with him. At mealtimes, he began rejecting even some of his favorite foods.

Three weeks later, a second attempt at screening took place in a conference room. He did somewhat better this time, doing well on non-verbal tests—when he felt like doing them. "After 2 hours he was angry and throwing the blocks at the therapist." At the end of the session, the team evaluating him said that Joshua's problems went beyond speech and perhaps included autism. His mother was devastated—and now felt guilty about punishing him for behavior which he might not be able to help.

A third evaluation session by this team took place at home. This time "Joshua was very polite and happy, calling them by name, repeating words, very cooperative with them." He took them to his room, showed them his toys and played with them. Although he prefers to wear only underpants, this time he wore clothes. After this complete turnaround, the evaluation team began to back away from the "autism" diagnosis. They approved his going to preschool.

This was both a relief and a new source of anxiety. How would Joshua respond to being on a school bus full of children who were strangers to him, and to being buckled into his seat by strangers? His parents asked for a prayer at their church that Joshua could be able to go to school.

When time came to get on the school bus, Joshua got on,

let himself be buckled in and did not whimper, cry, or even look sad as the bus drove away. He loved the school and his teacher said that she had no trouble with him. He even became sociable and would kiss people on the cheek. His mother said, "I don't know *what* changed, how it happened, *when* he changed," but "he is a totally different child from the one I reared for almost 4 years."

Joshua was perhaps the most striking example of children who suddenly do something when they are ready. This seems to have been his pattern with his learning letters and numbers, toilet-training, and his becoming mature enough to behave himself in a social setting. Unfortunately, the timetables of experts and the necessities of institutions do not adjust easily to the fact that different children become ready at different times.

Jonathan in New York

Jonathan was born in October 1989 and so was five years old when his mother first wrote to our group in December 1994. At that time, he was described as someone who "draws very well and has a photographic memory" but who "has great difficulty putting more than three words together" and "can't talk about abstract things." For example, "I can't ask him how was school today." His overall IQ was in the normal range at 97, but that average concealed an extreme variation between a much higher than normal non-verbal IQ of 136 and a much below normal verbal IQ of 70.

As an infant, Jonathan was "a very sleepy baby." He sat up at 7 months and walked at 14 months but "he did not babble as a baby." By the age of two, "I was concerned that he was not talking and could not even call me 'mommy.'" In this case, neither Jonathan's pediatrician nor others seemed as worried as his mother, who was told that boys are slower to develop.

Socially, Jonathan "always liked to parallel play with other children, but could not attend a nursery school or any group activity" because he "would be off doing his own thing." He "was slow to understand things all kids understand," his mother said. For example, Jonathan "didn't understand about opening up gifts." He was also clumsy and would trip over his own feet at two and a half years of age. However, he was "an extraordinarily affectionate child. He never seems to get enough from us. He's always hugging and kissing us. He's been a doll to raise." The only problem was talking: "I tried my best at $2\frac{1}{2}$ to get him to speak, but failed."

By age 4, however, Jonathan had a 50-word vocabulary and this rapidly increased by age 5 to a normal-sized vocabulary for his age, though he did not have the normal facility in using it. His speech at age 5 was "about where a $2\frac{1}{2}$ to 3 year old would be." In general, his development "is characterized by lags and spurts," his mother said. Within the six months prior to her writing our group, "he has gained 2 years in vocabulary" and in three months he went from being unable to draw a circle to drawing at a level more than a year ahead of his chronological age.

Preschool officials labelled him a high-functioning "autistic" child with "pervasive developmental disorder." However, a psychiatrist at Yale University disagreed with that diagnosis of Jonathan. "He was too friendly, socially appropriate, cognitively intact and learning too quickly to be in that group." Jonathan is also "the kind of child who is very aware of people in distress and loves animals," his mother said. Most people notice nothing unusual about him "until they talk to him and even then he can fake conversation with a lot of 'uh-huh's' and 'oh yes'!" At this point, at age five, Jonathan was attending a special education kindergarten in his school district.

His mother concluded: "So here I am, afraid he'll never be 'normal' or be able to get on in the world. Yet he's doing well at taking care of himself right now at 5. My fear is he'll never learn anything beyond concrete language and not be able to understand the abstract. Yet he scores well on the abstract portions of IQ tests. We never knew he didn't understand us or what we were saying. He was so good at picking up visual cues and body language that he faked us out . . . How can you tell how much a child understands if they can't speak well?"

Nearly two years passed before Jonathan's mother wrote to the group again in September 1996. Now she reported "incredible progress" but also that he still "has far to go." His verbal IQ had "gone up two standard deviations" and had now reached the lower end of the normal range, while his non-verbal IQ remained well above normal, giving him a higher overall IQ than before. The only way to tell that he still has problems is by trying "to have an in-depth conversation," where his problems with tenses, syntax, and pronouns come out. "The major thing that has happened in two years is I finally have a kid I can communicate with. He is capable of answering all sorts of questions and he asks all sorts of questions," though he "still has trouble with very abstract language." She plans to take him back to Yale for another evaluation in the spring of 1997. "Unfortunately," she says, in the meantime she has to deal with some "local authorities in the school system," and they remain fixated on the "pervasive developmental disorder" label, even though a psychiatrist and a neurologist shot that down two years ago.

Socially, Jonathan has "become very friendly toward other

children, although he doesn't always know what to say. He will play some games with other kids, but his language keeps him from understanding all the rules." His older sister, age ten, "has been a big help in the play area." He has learned how to pretend, "but doesn't do it often."

At school, Jonathan is still in a special education class, but one at "the highest level," and one which has one teacher and two assistant teachers for eleven children. "Many of the children in his class have average to high IQs, yet have language or learning disorders. He mainstreams for gym, library, art and music. Art continues to be his strong point. He draws beautifully." Although Jonathan was late in talking, he began reading at the age of three and a half. "Somehow language didn't make sense for him until he could see the words," his mother says. "It still helps him and he writes better than he speaks."

At school, Jonathan has "gone from being a child who didn't pay attention to the teacher to one who loves school and has great eye contact with everyone." At home, he receives multivitamin tablets which his mother says has "helped him enormously." He is "much more normal on vitamins and deteriorates when he's not on them."

Overall, "much has changed in two years," his mother says. "I realize my son is different, but I wouldn't trade him for the world." She recalls having said, two years earlier, that she couldn't even ask him what he did in school that day. "Now he comes home and tells me he doesn't want to talk about that right now!"

Kevin Michael in Alabama

Since there are two boys named Kevin in our group, the middle name of the one in Alabama will be added, so that he is Kevin Michael. He was born in June 1989 by cesarean delivery, weighing 9 pounds, 10 ounces and having a very large head.

Kevin's mother described him as "a sweet, playful baby" but one easily frightened by loud people or toys like jack-in-the-box. He was also afraid of elevators and public rest rooms. He has also become an increasingly finicky eater and refuses to eat brands of food—or even chocolate—that are different from what he is used to. His parents became concerned at an early age when he did not respond to directions as other toddlers did, nor wave bye-bye, or nod or shake his head. By the time he was two and a half years old, he had a vocabulary of about 20 words, but these were not used to ask for anything. He would say "cold" when he touched something cold and he could say "no." In fact, when he was taken to a center for developmental and learning disorders, he said "no" and pushed away all test materials.

Like other children in our group, Kevin Michael has been late in being toilet-trained, achieving this only around the time of his fourth birthday. As with the other children, it was not that he did not understand. He simply showed no desire to change his pattern of wearing diapers. Only after his parents stopped putting diapers on him did he discover that underpants were not doing the job—and then he decided to use the toilet.

Unlike some other children in our group, Kevin Michael not only was slow to use language himself but was largely unresponsive to other people's statements or questions and did not follow directions. When he was about three and a half, his mother took him to a neurologist for evaluation. Although he showed such patterns as becoming engrossed in watching things spin, as autistic children often do, the neurologist said that he was definitely not autistic. The neurologist also diagnosed him as having normal intelligence. Other possibilities of biological problems in the brain were left open, pending more sophisticated tests. Kevin was so upset at having gel being put in his hair so that electrodes could be used to monitor his brain activity that it took an hour to get 5 usable minutes of results. "It was almost impossible," his mother said afterwards. The results themselves showed no abnormality but a longer session would be needed—and this has been postponed until he is older and better able to cooperate.

Meanwhile, Kevin has been in special programs for speech therapy and socialization. His mother found that this "really seems to have made him happier and more responsive to what we say to him." When he was three years old, his speech was at the level of "Mommy turn on TV" or "Kevin ride Merry Go Round" or simply "Apple juice!" He still did not use pronouns, however. Nevertheless, Kevin's speech development was more advanced than my son's was at the same age.

Unlike some of the other children in our group who have been behavior problems, Kevin Michael is described by his mother as "a sweet boy who is very easy to have around" and someone "very gentle with household objects and toys." His parents noticed no special talents such as some other youngsters in our group have had. But, as he approached his fourth birthday, his mother reported that his memory was "amazing." When served a certain kind of meat, Kevin said, "At Brookwood Mall." More than a year earlier, he had had the same kind of meat at that shopping center. Still, his social skills were lagging. "Socially," his mother said, "he likes to play near other children and to have them chase him or play in a big box, but he doesn't respond to what they say to him and he doesn't even begin to understand more advanced games." However, his speech therapist says that what he has accomplished in a few months is what some other children have taken years to learn. Whether this rapid catching-up will continue only the future will tell. In the summer of 1996, Kevin's mother wrote: "Now, at age six, he is in a regular kindergarten class, doing good work, and it is obvious that he learns some things faster than the others. His problems continue to be in receptive language."

Not long afterwards, near the end of September 1996, she added: "Once diagnosed as 'developmentally delayed,' a term which I thought was a politically correct way to say mentally retarded, he's now one of the best readers in his class and asks questions about how he'll drive a car and where he'll work 'when I'm a big man.' It's hard to believe he was so delayed and was once 'deaf' to speech. The biggest change started soon after his fifth birthday, when he entered public kindergarten in a regular class with a wonderful teacher who truly loved him and wanted him in her class. She's one of the 'old-fashioned' teachers, who runs a structured classroom, so in spite of Kevin's language difficulties he always knew what he was supposed to be doing. At five, when he began kindergarten, he still did not acknowledge what other children said to him, although he usually responded to adults. The children in his class loved him and always took his hand to make sure he was a part of whatever they were doing. He soon learned to talk to them in a normal way."

Because Kevin turned six during the summer, he would have been eligible to enter the first grade in the fall of 1995, but his mother requested that he repeat kindergarten instead and the school agreed to let him do so. This second year of kindergarten "made such a difference in him," his mother said. "He had the same wonderful teacher, and she began 'backing off' helping him so much. He began to do much of his work independently, and the children in this class, some nearly a year younger than him, didn't even realize that he was a 'special case.' He still received speech therapy and occupation therapy in the classroom, but many of the children had their own little problems such as crying, hyperactivity, etc., so he was considered just one of the class."

When the second year of kindergarten ended in 1996, "that amazing teacher delivered to me a boy who could read and write sentences, speak in paragraphs, and act 'normal' wherever we went." There still remains the problem of how well he responds to what he hears from others, so his parents have requested "that he be provided with visual cues as necessary and written directions. They recognize that this might be a continuing problem but they are still very pleased with how far he has come. As of September 1996, "he was doing satisfactory work for a first-grader." The extra year he spent in kindergarten paid off big and the fact that his parents asked for it, instead of letting him go ahead when he might not have been ready, may make a lifetime of difference.

Andy in New York

Andy was born in April 1992. He was a year and a half old when he first said "dada," which may be either a word or just a sound, depending on whether the child is trying to convey anything by it. At about that time, he was taken to a speech therapist for four sessions a week, 30 minutes each. Andy was three and a half years old when he first made a statement using more than one word. Yet he was still not talking in the sense of speaking in sentences or engaging in back-and-forth conversation. When he was evaluated at a language center, a month before his fourth birthday, his language development was judged to be that of a child between a year and 18 months old.

In addition to being late in talking, Andy was a behavior problem, doing calculatingly disruptive things, tailored to what he could get away with with a particular person or in a particular situation. For example, "he'll try things at home when I am not here that he'd dare not do when I was around." At school, he has become aggressive and will sometimes bite, pinch, or hit. He "goes from one thing to another, not staying on task for more than a few seconds. He loves to play with things he shouldn't, like the fan in the classroom, the VCR, the TV, the sink, the drinking fountain, etc."

While his mother was concerned about "his sneaky behavior," she also recognized that this "shows his thought processes are working ... and oh too well." She said: "He knows just whose chain to jerk and what he can get away with and with whom."

Andy's mother learned of our group on the Internet and joined in 1996. She then flew out to Texas from the east coast to meet with another mother in the group, through whom she learned of our existence. "We spent the weekend talking and crying about our children's future. We still E-mail each other every day and sometimes that just isn't enough so we pick up the phone. In three days she will be coming out to visit me. I can hardly wait!"

Meanwhile, Andy was completing a bad year in the language development program. His mother described the teachers there as "the most rude, nastiest and most insensitive" team of special education teachers she had ever met. "As an educator myself, and after spending a year with inner-city children in grades 5–8 plus special ed, I have NEVER treated students in the inhumane way Andy was treated," she says. "All I can say is thank goodness he didn't know . . . or did he? The worst part was I had no other place to turn. I could not have removed him from the program because he would have stopped receiving all of his services. So we toughed out the year and although we are at the same school we have a loving team now."

As of the time when his mother returned the survey questionnaire to me in mid-1996, Andy was still not really talking. She wrote then: "The underlying conclusion is that Andy will someday talk because we have heard him say words, but nobody has been able to conclude that one day he will be able to converse as an adult with adults."

Fortunately, the answer to this question seemed to come shortly thereafter. His mother now wrote back: "Andy did start speaking in sentences and his speaking rapidly improved." This coincided with the end of the school year with the teachers his mother had complained about. Now his mother says: "I find each day with Andy so amazing and each progressive step toward fluent speech is met with a sigh of relief. Tonight I checked on him after he had fallen asleep and his hands were locked together above his head and the Mother Goose book lay across his chest. My little professor fell asleep reading. So I did what any mother would do—I ran into my room, grabbed my camera and took a picture!"

Brother and Sister in Texas

The only other family in our group with two children who talked late have a boy and a girl. Their son was born in 1989 and their daughter in 1991. Both have impaired vision, due to a congenital optic nerve defect, and the boy is legally blind. An ophthalmologist who examined him said that children with impaired vision often talk somewhat later, but that the degree of his delay seemed unlikely to be caused by that.

When the son's mental ability was tested by the public school system at age 3, no special allowance or special arrangements were made to accommodate his impaired vision. Questions that he could not see well enough to answer were simply marked wrong and he ended up being assigned an IQ of 70, far below normal. This mindless procedure was enough for his mother to decide that her children would be educated in private schools. When tested at age 6, the boy's IQ was now in the normal range. Although declared to be legally blind, he can see the letters on a computer keyboard.

Both children are described by their father—a third-generation engineer—as "bright, funny, sociable, and quite normal in most respects." His mother says, "If I had known how bright and articulate my son would turn out to be, I would have saved myself many years of anxiety." However, this experience helped her later to cope with her daughter's late talking: "I am confident she will show the same degree of improvement that her brother has shown."

This couple is unique in having the successful experience of one late-talking child to guide them in later dealing with another. Most parents of bright, late-talking children do not even know of any other child like theirs, much less have personal experience to draw on. To some extent, this sketch of such children in our group is intended to serve as a substitute.

three

Patterns in
the Group

A S A RESULT OF READING THE LETTERS THAT CIRCULATED WITHIN our group and talking with various parents on the phone, I began to think that there might be a pattern among these children and their families. Little did I suspect how striking that pattern would turn out to be! However, before looking at the patterns that emerged from our questionnaires, it is worth noting that this group may not be at all typical of late-talking children in general. First of all, the letters that came in were in response to newspaper columns which discussed not only my son's delayed speech development but also his remarkable memory and analytical abilities. Many of the parents wrote that their children were similar in these respects as well. Moreover, the parents I spoke with on the phone struck me as above average in intelligence—a conclusion supported, as I later discovered, by their educational and occupational levels. All this is worth emphasizing so as not to offer false hopes, which can be as cruel in their consequences as despair that is uncalled for.

First in 1994 and again in 1996, I sent out questionnaires to the parents in the group. The second questionnaire incorporated questions already asked in the first, as well as new questions based on my reading and reflections since the first survey. The second questionnaire was also sent out in part because the group had grown so much that many of the current members had not been part of the group during the first survey. Forty-four families, out of the 55 families in the group, filled out and returned the questionnaires that had been sent to them. These 44 families contained 46 late-talking children because of the two families which each had two such children. Their ages varied greatly. Seven of the late talkers are no longer children and the oldest is in his late forties. The youngest had not yet turned four at the time of the survey.

The later and larger 1996 survey is the one being reported here in detail, though the 1994 survey turned up very similar patterns. Both in 1994 and in 1996, the responses to the surveys showed striking patterns in the families of these children, as well as in the children themselves. Let us begin, however, at the beginning, with the most basic questions about these children: What is talking and when is it late?

———————

Talking is harder to define than it might seem to be at first glance, and several questions in the survey attempted to pin it down. The first of these questions asked when the child spoke his first word. But is "dada" or "mama" a word or just a sound? If the child uses it to convey some meaning, then it is a word. However, the questionnaire did not go into all that, so the answers to this particular question may not be quite as informative as intended. In any event, that first word (or sound) came somewhere around age two for about half the children in our group. By the age of three, three-quarters of the children (according to 32 out of 43 parents who remembered) had spoken this first word, or made this first sound. Clearly not all parents considered this to be "talking," or the five who said their first word or sound before they were a year old would never have been in a group of late-talking children, nor probably would many of the other parents whose children made such sounds in their early years.

Sometimes the first word was the only word spoken for a very long time. One boy said "mama" at six months, but then stopped saying it at ten months—and it was three years later before he spoke another word: "up." For all these reasons, the first word may not mean as much as in some other situations, where it is just the beginning of a continuous and growing process.

When did these children make their first statement using more than one word? More than half (59 percent) made statements containing more than one word by the time they were four. Among those who were earlier, 13 made statements of more than one word before their third year and another 11 did so during that third year, but 11 waited until the fourth year. However, three of the children in our study did not go beyond a single word until they were five years old and another five children had not yet reached the stage of saying two words when the 1996 survey was conducted. Saying more than one word at a time might seem like the beginning of real talking but, again, how often it happened is also a factor— and, unfortunately, not one I asked about. Some parents indicated that their child spoke very seldom and this may also have been true of some others.

A complete sentence was achieved by most of the 44 children for whom we had data by the time of the 1996 survey, although 7 had not yet reached this stage. Their fourth year was the most common time for them to speak their first sentence. Of the 37 who spoke in complete sentences, 11 did so before they were four years old, 20 by the time they were four and a half, and 17 afterwards. Only one child in our group reached this level before the age of three, while 10 waited until they were five years old or older before speaking their first complete sentence.

What is most clearly talking—back-and-forth-conversation—had also been achieved by 37 of the 44 children for whom we have data on this. Again, age four and a half was roughly the median. Twenty conversed earlier and 18 conversed later, with 14 doing so only in their fifth year. These conversations are not necessarily in complete grammatical sentences but they are conversations. Whether measured by complete sentences or by back-and-forth conversation, more of the children in our group began talking at age four than at any other age. But there is still a spread.

As might be expected, even after beginning to talk, many of the children in our group did not talk with as much skill or sophistication as children who had begun talking years earlier. However, those late talkers who have grown up achieved normal speech while still in childhood. It is of course a subjective judgment as to where they are at any given point along the way. I can recall being on the phone with the mother of a late-talking boy and hearing him speaking very plainly in the background. When the mother nevertheless expressed continuing concern about the level of his speech, I could not help wondering to myself: "What does she want from the kid—the Gettysburg Address?"

At what point did most parents think that their children were late in talking and what caused them to be seriously concerned at that point? While medical and scientific books may contain statistical averages and developmental "norms," based on what most children in the general population do, the question of when the child's lag in talking is a matter of concern is ultimately a subjective judgment and it has varied greatly from parent to parent in our group. Four parents were seriously concerned before their child was 18 months old but one was not seriously concerned until the child was five years old. However, for most of the children in our group—35 out of 46—their parents reported themselves as seriously concerned by the time the child was three years old and not yet talking. Eleven became seriously concerned only after the child's third birthday. Of the 40 families who reported using a speech therapist, the largest number—19— did so between the ages of two and three. However, in three cases, the parents waited until the child was five years old to begin speech therapy.

What first made the parents of the children in our group concerned? In most cases, the primary reason for concern was *not* the practical problems growing out of the child's non-communication. Only one parent gave that as the primary reason for being seriously concerned. Another four listed the child's own frustration or unhappiness as the primary reason. But by far the most common reason was that the usual time to talk had come and gone. Thirty-one parents cited this as their primary reason and, even among the 10 others who cited yet another reason, often that other reason was based on doctors or relatives who pressed home the point that it was now past the normal time for a child to be talking.

The most unexpected—indeed, startling—discovery from the survey of our group was that in 60 percent of these families the child had an engineer as a close relative. This had a particular impact on me because my brother is an engineer.

By "close relative" is meant either parents, grandparents, uncles, or aunts of the late-talking child. This does not include cousins and it does not count the closest relatives of all, the children's siblings, whom I neglected to ask about. However, for the younger children, this is unlikely to be a major omission, since most of these siblings are unlikely to be old enough to be pursuing careers. In these statistics about family background, only 43 families are counted, since one of the children was adopted and his biological family background is unknown.

Among the minority of children in this group who did not have an engineer among their close relatives, most had close relatives in other professions requiring high levels of analytical ability. The second questionnaire listed scientists, mathematicians, computer specialists, pilots, accountants, and physicians, as well as engineers, among the occupations to check and also contained a category for "other analytical" occupations, which the parent was to specify, so that I could determine whether this qualified as one requiring much analytical ability. The only two relatives in this category who were counted as analytical were both economists. Altogether, 86 percent of the families had a close relative of the child working in at least one of these occupations. Engineers, mathematicians, and scientists alone were found in 74 percent of these families. In addition, accountants were second only to engineers as the most frequent occupation. They were among the close relatives of the late-talking child in 54 percent of the biological families. These are the numbers of *families* with such relatives. The total number of engineers, accountants, etc. was often even larger than this might suggest, as a table will show in due course.

Another very striking discovery was that most of the children in this group had at least one close relative who played a musical instrument. There was at least one such person among the close relatives of the late-talking child in 81 percent of the families and more than one person who played a musical instrument in 60 percent of such families. Some were even professional musicians in 28 percent of these families. Here again, my personal experience was in keeping with these group patterns, since my father played the piano, as did his brother and sister. Some of the more striking examples among the families in the group included one where the child's father, grandfather, and two uncles were all engineers, while the mother and another grandfather were geologists, two aunts were accountants and two uncles played musical instruments. In another family, the father and both grandfathers were engineers, the mother was a computer specialist, and she, an aunt and an uncle all played musical instruments, the uncle professionally. The father was also a pilot.

The educational and ethnic patterns of the parents of late-talking children were not as striking as the prevalence of analytical and musical individuals in these families as a whole. However, the patterns among the parents are also interesting. Of the 70 parents for whom we have educational data, 51 have either college or postgraduate degrees and 14 more have had some college. While 91 percent of the biological mothers and 86 percent of the biological fathers are white, the non-white parents are similar to the white parents in being in analytical and/or musical occupations. Of the three black fathers, for example, two are economists and one is a professional musician. The one Asian father is a chemist and his wife, who is white, is a computer specialist.

The children themselves have very striking patterns. Of the 46 late-talking children in this survey, 39 are male. For the group as a whole, including those who did not fill out their questionnaires, 87 percent of the children are male. However, the seven females have patterns very similar to those of their male counterparts, both in their families and in themselves. For example, in five of the six families with girls who talked late, these girls have a close relative who is an engineer and in four of the six families the girls have accountants and musicians as close relatives.

Among the children themselves, one of the most striking patterns was their memories. Of the five categories of memory, ranging from "very poor" to "extremely good," more than half the children were rated in the highest category. Nearly three-fifths (59 percent) of the children were rated as having an extremely good memory, with all the rest being rated as having "above average" memories and none being ranked as low as "average." Among those given the highest rating, some parents wrote in additional comments, ranging from an exclamation point to "truly unbelievable." Another wrote: "His memory is better than any child I have spoken to," and said "other family members and teachers comment on it often." His memory for detail, his mother says, "is often better than my own." Similarly with ability at solving puzzles, 31 of the children (two-thirds) were ranked in the highest category—"unusually good"—while only 6 were "average," 5 "below average" and for 4 the parents had not noticed how they did with puzzles.

These general patterns applied to both girls and boys. But although the girls were similar to the boys in these respects, they were not particularly boyish otherwise. Only one out of the seven girls preferred toys for boys, while four out of seven preferred toys for girls, and one had no preference. Similarly, these girls showed no preferences for male playmates. Of six girls for whom this information was available, five showed no preference and one had only boys available to play with. The only late-talking girl I have heard of outside the group seemed similar in her mental development patterns to children of both sexes within the group. According to a newspaper story, she graduated 13th in her high school class of 700 in New Hampshire and was planning to specialize in engineering in college—and her father is an engineer.[1]

There were extremely few records of intelligence test results available. For the younger children, still lagging in speech development, there were some large disparities between verbal and non-verbal results in the few cases where data were available. Among the late talkers who had progressed beyond the stage of speech problems, three of those who had taken the Scholastic Aptitude Test all scored well above the 90th percentile on the mathematics portion of the test.

Another pattern among our group of children was delayed toilet-training. While most children are toilet-trained between two and three years of age, only 8 of the 44 children for whom we have this information were toilet-trained for urination before their third birthday. Nineteen became toilet-trained in this respect during their third year, 10 at age four and 4 at age five or later, while three were not yet toilet-trained at the time of the survey. For bowel movements, the distribution is very similar. The children in this group tended also to lag in social development. Most were ranked either "below average" (20) or "far below average" (12) in this respect as children. Among other things, this lends weight to above-average parental rankings of the same children in memory or puzzles, for it indicates that these parents were not simply making over-optimistic assessments in general.

When ranking their children's physical skills as well, most parents rated their children either average (18) or clumsy (12).

While a certain social ineptness fits the stereotype of "nerds," it is not at all clear that the below-average social skills of the late-talking children in this group are permanent characteristics, rather than what might be expected in youngsters still lagging in their ability to talk and perhaps self-conscious because of being different from other kids in that respect. Among the half-dozen late talkers who were rated on their social skills as adults, only one was rated below average and none far below average. Three were rated above average, one far above average and one average. However, this raises another question that applies more broadly: Will the young children in this group be like the adults when they reach the same ages?

If the late-talking children in this group are a biased sample of late-talking children in general, because of the way people responded to newspaper columns about my son and then about similar children whose parents formed the group, this bias might be even more pronounced among parents of late talkers who are now grown. By the very nature of the case, we cannot know today how the young ones will eventually turn out, but only the parents of adult late talkers who turned out well seem likely to write. I cannot recall receiving a single letter from a parent whose late-talking child turned out to be retarded, autistic, or otherwise suffering from a serious disability in adulthood, while at least a couple of the parents of young children in our group have subsequently learned that their child's misfortunes extend well beyond talking late. In short, the older late talkers may represent a more successful sample than the younger ones and both may represent a more successful sample than late-talking children in the general population.

The fact that we may—and probably do—have a biased sample of late-talking children in general does not invalidate what we have found nor limit its importance for those particular children to whom those findings apply. What it shows is that there is a very clear pattern of mental abilities and family backgrounds for a particular subset of late-talking children and that parents and people in the medical, educational and child-care professions would do well to be aware of them.

In addition to the overall group statistics, it may be useful to look at the individual profiles of the same children, listed here only by an identification number and sex, in order to preserve their privacy. The age of talking will be defined here, for the sake of consistency, as the earliest age at which either complete sentences were spoken or back-and-forth conversation occurred, even though isolated words or two or three-word phrases might have been spoken before. The late talkers shown below have been given numbers for identification and are listed in chronological order by age, with the first seven being college age or older.

NUMBER	SEX	FAMILY	AGE OF TALKING	MISCELLANEOUS
1	Male	grandfather and aunt played musical instruments	5 years old	unusually high I.Q.
2	Male	uncle an engineer, grandfather a chemist; another uncle an accountant	3 years old	parents told not to expect him to talk
3	Male	uncle an engineer, father an economist, grandfather played piano	nearly 4 years old	scored over 90th percentile on mathematics SAT
4	Male	brothers play music professionally, mother played music	cannot remember	degree in computer science
5	Male	two uncles accountants and one uncle a physician; father an economist	age 4	scored over 90th percentile on mathematics SAT
6	Female	uncle an engineer; father and an uncle computer specialists; grandfather a mathematician; mother and 2 aunts accountants	3 years old +	I.Q. well above average
7	Male	father and aunt play musical instruments	cannot remember	scored over 90th percentile on mathematics SAT
8	Male	grandfather an engineer, father a computer specialist and plays musical instrument	3 years, 8 months	when a toddler, he could assemble jigsaw puzzles with 100 to 250 pieces
9	Female	grandfather and uncle engineers; both parents, a grandmother, and an uncle and aunt all play musical instruments	4 years old	an identical twin
10	Female	grandfather and uncle engineers; both parents, a grandmother, and an uncle and aunt all play musical instruments	4 years old	an identical twin
11	Male	two grandfathers and two uncles engineers; one uncle a computer specialist; father an accountant; both parents play musical instruments	3 years old	youngest child in family

12	Male	grandfather an engineer; an uncle a scientist; an aunt and uncle play music	between 5 and 6	is being home schooled
13	Male	adopted in a foreign country and family history unknown	between 4 and 5	in regular public school
14	Male	uncle a computer specialist; grandmother plays music	4 years old	"gradual improvement" in speaking
15	Male	father, grandfather and two uncles engineers; mother and other grandfather geologists; two aunts accountants; two uncles play musical instruments	5 years old	vision severely impaired
16	Male	uncle an accountant	not yet talking at age 7	speaks many words but not yet back-and-forth conversation as of September 1996
17	Male	father a chemist; mother a computer specialist; a grandfather and an uncle physicians; both parents, a grandfather and an uncle play musical instruments	4 years old	mental ability in normal range
18	Male	one uncle an engineer; another a computer specialist; grandfather and an uncle play musical instruments	4½ years old	excels in spelling and computers
19	Male	father a computer software engineer; grandfather an accountant; both parents and an aunt play musical instruments	6 years old	academically at or above grade level
20	Male	father a musician; one uncle a computer specialist; an aunt and two other uncles accountants	not yet talking at age 6	younger of two brothers
21	Male	father and both grandfathers engineers; mother a computer specialist; father also a pilot; mother, aunt, and an uncle play musical instruments, the uncle professionally	5½ years old	non-verbal I.Q. well above normal; verbal I.Q. in normal range
22	Male	grandfather an engineer; grandmother plays musical instrument	6 years old	especially likes computers

23	Male	one uncle an engineer, another a scientist, and an aunt an accountant	age 5	sudden improvements
24	Female	mother, grandmother, grandfather, aunt and uncle all play musical instruments	nearly 5 years old	seems intelligent and observant
25	Male	uncle an engineer; grandfather an accountant;both parent, a grandfather and an aunt play musical instruments	3½ years old	mental test scores above average
26	Male	grandfather an engineer; father and an uncle accountants; another uncle a physician; mother, grandmother, grandfather and an aunt play musical instruments	4½ years old	rapidly catching up in talking
27	Male	grandfather an engineer; father and grandfather play musical instruments	not yet at age 6	only child in the family
28	Male	both parents trained in biology; grandfather accountant; father plays musical instrument	3 years old	I.Q. in normal range
29	Male	uncle a pilot; mother and grandfather play musical instruments	4 years old	no abnormalities accompanying speech delay
30	Male	uncle a computer specialist; father an accountant; mother, grandmother, grandfather, aunt play musical instruments	age 3	mental test results range from well above average in reading to slightly below normal range for non-verbal reasoning; computer skills "amazing"
31	Female	grandfather an engineer; father computer specialist; uncle an accountant	4½ years old	sudden recent improvement in speech
32	Male	uncle an engineer; mother, both maternal grandparents, and an uncle play musical instruments	3 years old	an only child

33	Male	an engineer and a pilot as grandfather(s); aunt is accountant; mother, grandmother, 4 aunts, 2 uncles and grandfather play musical instruments, most professionally	2¼ years old	"an intense interest in details. . .very organized"
34	Male	father a pilot; grandmother an accountant	4 years old	a number of medical problems
35	Male	mother, aunt, and uncle play musical instruments, the uncle professionally	3½ years old	"now, he is talking all the time"
36	Male	father and grandfather engineers; grandfather a pilot; father plays musical instrument, sometimes professionally	2½ years old	mental ability tested in normal range
37	Male	father and grandfather engineers; two aunts and an uncle biochemists; father, two aunts and an uncle play musical instrument and the uncle teaches music	"not yet" in September 1996	does some sign language
38	Male	father an engineer and plays musical instrument	age 4	youngest of 3 children
39	Female	grandfather an engineer; another grandfather and three uncles are computer specialists; both parents have bachelor's degrees in science; mother, grandmother, and two uncles play musical instruments, one uncle professionally	just over 4 years old	an only child, IQ in normal range
40	Female	father, grandfather and two uncles engineers; mother and other grandfather geologists; two aunts accountants; two uncles play musical instruments	3½ years old	older brother talked late also, so parents are more able to cope
41	Male	grandfather an engineer; mother and two uncles accountants	4 years old	an only child
42	Male	two uncles are computer specialists, another a mathematician, and another a physician; an aunt is a marine biologist	nearly 4 years old	youngest child in the family

43	Male	father and two uncles are engineers; mother is a computer specialist; grandfather a mathematician;all five play musical instruments, as does another uncle	not yet talking at age 4½	"can operate any VCR, anywhere, anytime"
44	Male	grandfather and grandmother play musical instruments	4 years, two months old	began to talk after his questionnaire was returned saying that he was not talking
45	Male	grandfather and two uncles engineers; father a computer specialist; one uncle is a pilot and another a scientist; both parents play musical instruments, as do a grandmother and a grandfather, an aunt and an uncle	not yet at age 4	very limited vocabulary but it is growing
46	Male	father and an uncle are accountants and an aunt plays a musical instrument professionally	not yet at age 3½	first-born child in the family

If we were to summarize for a "typical" child of our group, he began really talking at about age four, after having used isolated words earlier. The parent usually became concerned after the child turned two, not so much because of immediate practical problems caused by his lack of communication, but more because the time for beginning to talk had come and gone. The great majority of parents then sought professional help, usually from a speech therapist, at age two. The results were reported as good 73 percent of the time, but others reported no results, bad results, or doubtful results. However, even those who reported good results sometimes wondered if that was the effect of the therapy or of the child's natural development with the passage of time.

Most parents also had their child evaluated by medical or psychological specialists, often several times over a period of years. Exactly half of these first evaluations were reported as stressful for the child—sometimes very much so, but second evaluations were reported as predominantly non-stressful. The conclusions reached included "autistic" in 32 percent of the cases and some other disorder in another 32 percent. As we have seen, some of these diagnoses did not stand up over time and some of the professionals involved later backed away from their own earlier diagnoses. Moreover, some of the other "disorders" described seemed to be little more than a rephrasing of the fact that the child was late in talking. How all this will turn out in the long run, of course, only the future will tell. What we know right now is that we have a remarkable group of children with a very pronounced pattern among themselves and in their families.

four

Patterns
Outside the Group

Not all the late-talkers I learned about were in our group. Those outside the group include (1) children who talked late for a variety of reasons, having no necessary connection with the patterns found inside our group, (2) individuals whose late-talking was part of a pattern very similar to patterns found in our group, and (3) autistic children. Any discussion of late-talking children as a broad category will include all of these. Much research on late-talking children *as a broad category* compares them with "normal" children and often reaches dire conclusions.

Studies show that late-talking children as a broad category tend to have lower IQs and poorer academic performances, and to have other continuing problems when tested or evaluated years later. Children may talk late because they are deaf, mentally retarded, or autistic—or they may talk late without any of these problems or any other problem. When the broad category of late-talking children is more carefully broken down, the general pattern of subnormal intelligence or permanent problems with speech or reading, for example, does not apply to all the sub-groups.

A study in England, for example, found that among those children whose only problem at age three was simply that they did not talk, more than three quarters had a good outcome (as defined by that study) by age five and a half.[1] In contrast, among those children in the same study who could neither talk nor understand what was said to them, only 14 percent had good outcomes. Another study, in New Zealand, found that those who had a delay in either language expression or language comprehension at age three "were not a high-risk group for later problems" but that those who had both were.[2] A Canadian study came closest to focusing on children like most of those in our group. This study took young children (21 months to 41 months old), whose hearing was normal and whose mental test scores did not fall below the normal range, and followed them for two or more years, re-examining them when they were from four to seven years of age. The results were that "the children's total language skills have increased to the normal range, or at least to a level appropriate to their intellectual skills." Because these children did not have as much experience in talking as other children their ages, they had some remaining articulation problems "resembling those of children who talk earlier but develop similar articulation difficulties, albeit at an earlier age."[3] In other words, these late-talking children went through the same language difficulties as other children do when they first begin talking.

In short, there are sharp differences among different categories of late-talking children. For some, it is just a passing phase and for others it is a harbinger of continuing trouble and other problems down the road. These studies suggest that children who can neither speak nor understand what is said to them are at much greater risk than children who are simply delayed in talking. As the authors of the Canadian study note, even before doing their study, their years of clinical experience with children with "simple developmental speech delay" had "suggested a favorable prognosis for speech within a few years, certainly by the age of school entry." They quote another authority who said, "The majority of these children with normal subsequent language development will have no easily identifiable speech disorder by the age of seven or eight years."[4]

For parents of late-talking children, the crucial question is: Which of these very different categories applies to my child? Parents cannot automatically assume that their children are like the children described in this book, for the danger that they may have other problems is not to be taken lightly—and false hopes may be cruel, not only in the disappointment they may lead to, but also in the neglect of treatment that might otherwise reduce the damage caused by a very serious condition. As the Canadian scholars did in their study, these parents need to check the hearing and the mental development of their children, as well as that can be determined by non-verbal tests administered by people with common sense. Neither all tests nor all testers are equally reliable, nor are all children sufficiently cooperative to make the results meaningful. Two children had to be dropped from the Canadian sample because of their "provocative and negative" behavior, much like the behavior of some of the children in our group.

In addition to late-talking children in the general population, there are late-talking children whom I have encountered personally at various times or have read about in popular publications or in letters from people who had heard of our group. These children are very likely a biased sample, biased toward the kinds of children in our group, since there would be no reason to bring to my attention children who were deaf, mentally retarded or autistic. Nevertheless these additional late-talkers may shed some light on the special subset of children we are focussing on—bright children whose speech development is delayed.

One such child was the son of a neighbor on the Stanford University campus—the neighbor being a mathematical economist. I lived in the neighborhood long enough to see the little boy grow out of his late-talking stage and show every sign of being a bright and alert child. Then there were other people whom I knew as adults, without knowing that they had been late-talking children until I mentioned our group to them. One was my old college roommate, who is chairman of the mathematics department at a well-known eastern college. His father was a graduate of M.I.T. Yet another was my colleague and friend Walter Williams, an economist at George Mason University. A lady who cut my hair also turned out to have a late-talking son—and her father was studying engineering when he left to go into military service during World War II. A colleague of my wife mentioned a surgeon who had talked late. In all these cases there was an analytical connection, as there was with my computer consultant mentioned in the first chapter. When I decided to write this book, I approached two publishers. The assistant to the head of one of these publishing houses then revealed that he had talked late. So did the owner of the other publishing house, who had been a professional violinist before going into publishing.

Just before this book went to press, I was visiting New Zealand and mentioned our group at a social gathering in the capital city of Wellington. The lady seated across from me at dinner immediately mentioned a boy she used to baby-sit for a friend. Not only did he talk late, despite being obviously bright, he was also late in toilet training. Today he is grown and an engineer. The next evening, at a gathering in the city of Dunedin, I mentioned our group again and a lady seated next to me said that her husband had talked late. He is a mathematician.

Only days before the final draft of this manuscript went to the publisher, I learned that one of my great nieces on the east coast had talked late and was in speech therapy for two years. By the time she was in junior high school, her mathematics ability had attracted enough attention for her to be tested for the program for mathematically precocious youth at Johns Hopkins University. Another late-talking youngster in my family was a nephew who was still speaking in a way that was so difficult for others to understand that, when time came for him to go into the public schools, his parents were fearful that he would be sent home. He was not—and he went on to earn a Ph.D. in mathematical economics at Princeton.

A letter from a reader in California said: "I was much interested in your column on children that don't talk until three or four years old. My father was one of them. My grandmother claimed that he just pointed and grunted until the age of three. However, he was far from retarded! He went from fairly humble beginnings to become one of Chicago's most respected lawyers (University of Michigan) and a wealthy man."

Another boy that I know of through family connections is unique in that his parents did not worry about him and did not take him to be tested for anything. He finally talked at about the same age as the children in our group, including those whose parents had moved heaven and earth to try to find out why he was not talking and how they could get him to speak. This youngster took readily to computers like a number of the children in our group and then became interested in playing chess.

All these were male, except for my great niece, so not only did the analytical pattern hold, so did the male predominance. A female late talker outside the group that I learned about from a newspaper clipping was the New Hampshire girl mentioned in Chapter 3 who was the daughter of an engineer and herself a high academic achiever. According to the story, "At age 3, she was the little girl who could not talk, not even to form the first, most basic baby sounds, 'mama and dada.'"

"You know how babies coo?" her mother said. "She never cooed."

As within our group, patterns found among late-talking males seemed to fit late-talking females outside the group. A letter from a grandmother who had read one of my columns about late-talking children told of a number of late-talking girls in her family, ranging across four generations.

"Although there have been many slow talkers in my family, the most dramatic case is one of my daughters—one of five children—who at the age of four was just beginning to say a few words and was not toilet trained. She was tested by a psychologist and found to be of low average IQ (which I took to be 80–90) and a dire academic future was forecast for her. There are many turns to this story, but the upshot is that I kept her back a year before starting her in first grade. From the first day of school she was a straight A student and graduated number one in her high school class of over 650. She was particularly skilled in math as were two of her sisters. She went on to earn her doctorate and is now a practicing psychologist . . ." Incidentally, the late toilet-training was something I had never mentioned in my writings about our group until now, so the fact that this was pointed out by the reader who wrote me is especially significant as showing a parallel with the children in our group.

A similar pattern re-appeared in the three and a half year old grand-daughter of the lady who wrote me. "Her IQ tests in the 70s except when non-verbal tests are used; then she tests 138. Her skills with puzzles and numbers is truly spectacular. A happy child, she is shy and does not speak much." Psychologists want to put the little girl in special programs but the family will not go along, in view of their history—at least not for now. "There is always time for special education later if it turns out that is what's needed in her case."

The dangers in an "early intervention" strategy include the school system's pigeon-holing the child for the future. As a man wrote to me about his late-talking nephew: "My concern is that without significant improvement over the next year, he will be placed in some sort of special education class, with appropriate federal funding, when he enters kindergarten. My own children's teachers have warned me that once that happens, it is extremely difficult to get a child back into a normal classroom." More may be involved here than mere dogmatism, for the school would lose federal money if the child were to be reclassified as normal.

One of the other dangers of early intervention was illustrated by the experience of a mother of a late-talking two-and-a-half-year old. A speech therapist helped him to develop a vocabulary of 20 words after about two months. Then she taught him sign language—and in two weeks "he stopped talking!" Experts "kept telling me it would help him in the long run and they had research studies to support this view." Against her better judgment, the mother went along with them, but her son "rarely said a word again until he was almost 4." Fortunately, another mother told her of a good speech therapist. Between the new therapist, a speech disorder center, and the passage of time, her son "has made incredible progress" and was now "a completely different child," not only in his improved speech but also in improved behavior, now that he was no longer so frustrated in trying to make his wants understood.

Not all professionals are advocates of "early intervention," however. In some cases, a doctor—especially a private physician with no axe to grind for the public school system—may counsel patience and it is the parents who are reluctant to wait for the child's development pattern to unfold. The parents of a late-talking two-and-a-half-year-old who were told to have patience "had visions of being told at age 4 or 5 that he had some kind of problem and had we acted sooner we could have saved him from falling behind his peers." Their description of him, however, seems to fit that of a child with a simple speech delay, without any problem with understanding: "He can follow a series of instructions and doesn't usually have much of a problem getting his point across using the few words he knows along with gestures."

The parents add: "What really interested us about your article was the connection between the children in the group being late talking and having family members with analytical and musical skills. My parents sing and my father plays a couple of difficult instruments. Nothing professionally speaking, just amateur performances in the community. My mother's family has a couple of trained musicians ... Our son loves music. He is constantly singing (not using words), playing his toy guitar and piano and using whatever objects he can as a drum."

A grandmother wrote me about her eight-year-old grandson who was late in talking "and in fact still does not talk well. He has been tested for a hearing deficit several times, but nothing was found. He is really quite smart and understands well all things around him. His math skills are on a par with those of his sister, who is 12."

The mother of three late-talking children began by describing her oldest, a seven-year-old boy who "barely talked at all until he was 4 years old, and then he talked in an atypical manner. He used scripted sentences he had heard on TV or elsewhere." Although this is a characteristic sometimes found in autistic children, "he was obviously not autistic" because he was "a loving and cheerful child." She adds: "Like many of the children you wrote about, Stephen has exceptional skill with the computer and a fantastic memory." Her daughter, age 4 "was also somewhat delayed in her language acquisition." She too began talking in a scripted manner, though "not as severely affected as her brother." She did not have the same analytical skills or memory as her brother but, like him, had intelligence test scores in the normal range. The youngest child, a daughter, "is also late-talking" but "does not script lines from elsewhere" and "uses original sentences." The children's family tree, sketched by the mother, includes an uncle in computer science and two other uncles who are physicians, as well as a grandfather who is an engineer.

Among those outside the group who wrote me were two whose children were now adults. One lady said that reading the column about my son "made my skin cover with goose bumps as you described my oldest son and our family." Her son "barely talked until he was four years old. But he walked at 9 months, showed good intelligence in all ways" so "no one ever questioned his ability because of his not talking." However, some did blame her "because I was at his beck and call and he didn't have to talk." As in other families, a brother talked much earlier, so it seems very unlikely that child-rearing practices were to blame for one child's late talking.

Like his father, this boy was very good "at any game with numbers involved." When tested as a student, he scored in the top 5 percent on mathematics problems. Now an adult, age 34 and married with two children, he "owns his own computer firm and does all the programming and consulting to keep the computers of various small companies running." His father was an engineer at IBM and his mother has three relatives who play the piano.

Another lady wrote about her grown son, who did not talk until he was two and a half years old. When his parents were decorating their Christmas tree, his mother kept exclaiming, "Isn't that pretty!" She was then surprised to hear her little boy say "pretty"—his first word—and his talking continued developing from there. Late in walking, he also began to do that suddenly and unexpectedly, without having crawled. He also displayed the independence and strong will characteristic of many of the children in our group. "If I tried to help him, he pushed me away."

Like many of the children in our group, "he was always good at puzzles." He also began reading when he was three. Later, in school, he scored a very high 149 on the IQ test. He was "a whiz at fixing things and making things electrical," with no help from his father, "who couldn't change a fuse in the box!" The son, however, became a ham radio operator at age ten, making his own sets from kits. "He almost seemed to put those kits together by instinct. He barely looked at the directions." In college he got married, graduated high in his class and went on to become a commercial airline pilot. His father, grandfather and uncle were all civil engineers and his mother a concert pianist—one of many musical people in her family.

It seems likely that these letters, like the letters that came from parents who joined our group, are a biased sample of late-talking children, since people whose children turned out badly may not have been nearly as inspired to write. This does not invalidate what was said by those who did, but it does suggest that such children may be exceptional among late-talkers in general and that they have a whole constellation of related characteristics, which deserves further study, if only to distinguish those who talk late for one reason from those who talk late for very different reasons and may have very different futures ahead of them.

Not all the letters from those outside the group contained such success stories and most of those within the group have no way of knowing how their children will turn out. One lady wrote: "My son is also language-delayed. But, unlike your son, he will never study computer science; at best, he will be the salad maker for Taco Bell. My son is eight years old and has Down's syndrome."

Finally, there was a boy I learned about from newspaper clippings, who talked late because he was autistic, but who nevertheless ended up far better off than most autistic youngsters. His story is worth exploring at some length below.

———————————

The word so much dreaded by many parents of late-talking children, and the label so freely applied by others (with and without the requisite qualifications or evidence) is "autistic." But even this dreaded term covers a range of conditions and potentialities. At the high end of that range is Trevor Tao, an Australian teenager of Chinese ancestry who has already made quite a mark in chess and in music. His story was told in a book published in Australia titled *The Opening Door* by Jean Bryant.

Trevor was diagnosed as autistic at the age of 2½. According to his mother: "He wasn't saying a word at that stage, didn't seem to understand our speech and showed signs of rocking, finger-watching and tantrums. However, his parents knew that Trevor was not deaf because he would spend hours absorbed in music, as well as in counting. The Autistic Children's Association sent a special teacher, Jean Bryant, to come and teach him five mornings a week." She gradually helped him integrate into a normal kindergarten and, later, primary school. Meanwhile, at home the family used various methods that had been developed for teaching autistic children how to read. When Trevor finally began to talk, his first words were those that he had already learned from flash cards.

In 1989, at the age of 11, Trevor gave an unusual musical performance—Dvorak's "New World Symphony" played on a piano, *without a note of music in front of him*. His music teacher, who at first did not want to accept an autistic child as a student, now describes Trevor as a genius and calls his memory "phenomenal." Trevor also became Australia's junior chess champion in 1992 at the age of 14 and, in 1994, moved up to join the top Australian chess players, finishing third in the national chess championship tournament at the age of 16.

These and other achievements came only after years of dedicated work by special education teacher Jean Bryant, who played a role in his development analogous to that of

Anne Sullivan in the development of Helen Keller. She never doubted that Trevor was autistic. He had "all of the symptoms," she says. Still, she found him "a very appealing toddler" when she first met him. Although she had worked with other autistic children as a volunteer helping someone else, Trevor was the first child she worked with on her own.

Unlike some "experts" who have all the answers, Mrs. Bryant says, "I am sure of nothing." She does not try to get others to follow her procedures and also says, "I do not wish to give false hope to the parents of children who have severe intellectual disability with their autism." Trevor Tao's autism was accompanied by high intelligence.

Teaching the little boy music, mathematics and reading was easy, for his abilities were already apparent in these areas before Mrs. Bryant arrived on the scene. It was in the social areas that he lagged far behind. In addition to not talking, he gave no indication that he heard, much less understood, what was said to him. Jean Bryant used the abilities he already had to help in other areas where Trevor was lagging. For example, she made use of his ability to read to give him written instructions on how to dress himself when he was five years old.

Even when Trevor repeated words in his early years, it was as sounds, for which he had both great ability and great interest as to intonation and rhythm. But he did not use words appropriately as words. He could learn nouns by reading them from cards containing pictures of what they stood for but that was not the same as being able to use them to get things or to express ideas or feelings. He had no apparent sense of the purpose of words—an inductive skill whose lack also made an understanding of social behavior difficult for him to achieve.

Trevor's social behavior remained at very primitive levels, with obsessions about some things and complete aversions to others. When he was two, he spent long periods of time spinning a ball or other objects and, after he learned about counting and music, he would spend hours on these activities. He was also obsessed with putting objects end to end, whether these were clothespins or colored pens. His aversions were equally strong. He hated being in a confined space, such as an elevator or a fitting room. He screamed uncontrollably and had tantrums. He also did not look directly at his parents, though he spent much time contemplating his outstretched fingers, and he was difficult to toilet-train. These were among the symptoms of autism, though some of these same actions are found among children who are not autistic. As Mrs. Bryant noted: "It is said that all of the 'autistic' behaviours are normal at some stage." It is apparently their persistence beyond that stage which marks autism.

After Trevor learned colors, he named them in an obsessive way. He would name the colors of his pens but showed no interest in, or awareness of, their function as pens.

In a sense, Jean had to become obsessive too, repeating new concepts until Trevor finally grasped what she was saying. For example, whenever they walked through the house opening doors and then closing them behind them, she verbalized this until finally—after months—he showed that he knew what the words meant. His phenomenal ability to learn concrete things was matched by a great slowness in learning new concepts or in transposing old concepts to new settings. When Jean suggested at kindergarten that Trevor should go to the toilet, for example, he snapped, "I do wee-wee at home!"

From an early age, Trevor seemed to have a photographic memory. As a toddler, he could repeat patterns of notes that his elder brother played on the piano and could play simple tunes after hearing them one time. When Jean played a harmonica with differently colored keys for each note and turned her back to Trevor, he would tell her the color of the note she was playing.

As Trevor slowly developed his ability to communicate, his tantrums declined and his behavior in general improved, suggesting that the frustration of trying in vain to make himself understood was part of the problem. His retrogression when he was sick likewise suggests a morale problem rather than an intellectual problem. Moreover, some of his autistic obsession patterns seemed to be a way of withdrawing from baffling and difficult situations into a familiar routine. Even when he was a baby, his parents found that sometimes counting to him when he was upset was the only way to calm him down.

There were no formulas that could be applied to developing little Trevor in the areas where he was behind. It was simply a test of ingenuity, of patience, of wills, and of energy. On some of the difficult early days, "I was usually glad to leave" when the time was up, Jean later admitted. Slowly, however, Trevor began to pick up subtle social concepts like "later" and to see how he was expected to behave in social situations. But, since he was learning all these things later than most children, just as he was talking later than most children, he was far behind them in his proficiency in both areas. This became painfully apparent when he entered kindergarten at age three and a half.

Jean went with him to kindergarten and was standing by when he needed her or when he just needed to be taken out of a situation to be by himself and regroup. The first crisis came on the first day of kindergarten when Trevor used the toilet and flushed it. This toilet was much louder than the one he was used to at home, causing him to scream at the top of his lungs as he backed out of the cubicle. His mother later told Jean that Trevor often had trouble with using new toilets. The next day, however, he joined some other boys playing with trains—until he heard a piano being played. Then he ran off to the piano, with a look of pleasure all over his face.

Although he was the youngest child in his preschool, Trevor was more advanced than most of the others in purely cognitive skills, though he was not nearly as advanced socially, especially in such nuances as reading body language. In Jean's words, he "missed the kind of communications cues that we took for granted."

While Trevor's speech at first tended to echo what was said to him, eventually he began to go beyond that and to initiate discussion with other children. He tried, not always successfully, to be one of them. His speech was still stilted. When there were large numbers of people to deal with, he tended to withdraw into himself and resume such autistic activities as scrutinizing his fingers.

Trevor's attempts to be more social involved watching what other children were doing, watching how Jean interacted with people, and trying to imitate. Even with something as basic as urinating in the toilet, he would often show the discomfort of needing to go, but wait until Jean told him to. Then he immediately took off his pants and did so. Apparently it was not that he did not know what to do physically, he just needed to be prompted socially.

When Trevor was four years and eight months old, he was given mental tests, which showed him to be at a four and a half year old level in verbal comprehension and at a two and a half year old level in verbal expression. There was little spontaneity or variety in his talk. He said what he had been more or less programmed to say in particular situations. "I could accurately predict often *the precise words* that Trevor would use in his replies," Jean later said. The painful slowness of his progress and the large gap between what he understood and what he needed to understand sometimes brought Jean close to despair and her health suffered from the stress.

Still, she kept at it and very slowly Trevor began to add some variety to his talk, while still using the stilted phrases he had committed to memory for particular situations. One of the signs of his social development was his looking directly at people more often and standing close to them—sometimes *too* close to other children, as he had no sense of their need for space.

One consequence of Trevor's greater interest in socializing with the children around him was that he made more *faux pas* and sometimes was rejected. Jean recalls her eyes filling with tears as she watched.

Whenever music was played in the kindergarten, Trevor's face would brighten. At home, he spent at least an hour a day playing the piano and was taking lessons. When the kindergarten staff realized that he could play the piano, they asked him to play for the class and he was very proud to do so. At the same time, he was still not using the toilet spontaneously but was waiting for Jean to tell him to go.

Jean tried to walk a fine line between being there for Trevor when he needed her and not letting him become so dependent on her that his own development lagged unnecessarily. At one point the director of the kindergarten mentioned that Trevor had begun to talk more with other children when she was not around. He also began to empathize with other children who cried by putting his arm around them. This caused Jean to begin to think that it was necessary to consider when it was time to let go. Trevor, by this time, was also aware that he was different—and he now resented being treated differently from other children.

When Trevor entered primary school—the first child from the Autistic Children's Association of South Australia to enter a regular class—he was initially overwhelmed but then began to progress socially as well as academically. He could now get up in class and talk about things he had done. Still, his development was uneven—and his frustration sometimes led to tears when he couldn't do things like put the lid on his lunch box properly and couldn't cut out pictures like the other children.

After six weeks of primary school, Jean bowed out and left Trevor on his own. However, she was gone for only a few months before she was asked to return. There were problems in school that the teachers could not cope with. In addition to social maladjustments, there were problems of comprehension in some kinds of situations. For example, he had trouble with irregular verbs, which did not fit the logical structure of his mind like mathematics or music. In some of the mathematics exercises, the children were supposed to pretend to be merchants making change for customers. Here Trevor did the math part fine but had trouble grasping the social mechanics of the situation. For this, Jean was able to help him where he lagged behind by building on what he excelled in. Trevor was very proud of his mathematics ability and smiled when the time of day came for him to leave his first-grade classmates to go to his math class with third and fourth graders.

Unlike some other autistic children who were withdrawn from the confusing world of social relations into the predictable little world of their own eccentric activities, Trevor was on the jagged edge between the two worlds. Aware that he was different while trying so much—and sometimes so unsuccessfully—to be part of the social life of the children around him, Trevor was sometimes found by teachers to be crying on the playground because he had no one to play with. Again, sometimes with painful slowness, Jean was able to help his social development along. A landmark came when he was invited to another boy's birthday party. In school, Trevor was becoming able to express himself more—telling classmates about going to a concert with his family and other personal experiences.

As before, progress was mixed with retrogressions. Sometimes he would burst into tears for no apparent reason. Investigation usually brought out that he had been singled out for some special treatment that reminded him of how different he was. Sometimes on the playground he was the butt of children's cruel remarks, whether for his unusual behavior or simply because his Asian appearance was different from theirs. Still, the progress continued in its uneven way and once again it became time for Jean to bow out of his life, this time for good.

Chess and music became increasing social outlets for Trevor. A chess set in the school library enabled him to escape the loneliness at lunch breaks and his music classes outside of school put him in the midst of other children with interests like his own. When Jean returned as a visitor to his home one day to watch his little music group performing, she saw Trevor interacting well in this setting, as he provided piano accompaniment to other precocious children playing violins.

Trevor's musical talents began to receive more public notice, including a television program appearance and a special concert, by invitation only, attended by the governor of the state of South Australia and other dignitaries. This concert was the first of many. In 1991, he won first prize in a music composition contest, one of many awards he was to win in both chess and music.

After a passage of years, Jean decided to write a book about Trevor and returned to the Tao home to be brought up to date on his accomplishments and his social progress. By now, at age fifteen, Trevor remembered very little from the years when Jean had worked with him. But his social progress showed the fruits of it. He was still shy and sometimes eccentric but he was not only coping but achieving.

In international chess competitions, Trevor Tao obtained a chess rating among the top one thousand players in the world. At the Moscow chess Olympiad in 1994, he played an American grandmaster to a draw. In 1995 he won a bronze medal in the international mathematics olympiad, held in Toronto. In 1996, he began studying at the University of Adelaide for a science degree in mathematics and computer science and a music degree with a double major in piano performance and composition.

While the strengths and weaknesses of Trevor Tao—and some other autistic children—bear a chilling resemblance to some of the strengths and weaknesses of many of the children in our group, there is another group to which many of our children bear a resemblance—that of high-IQ individuals in general. There are still other groups whose patterns strongly suggest a biological basis for their distinctiveness. One that is the opposite of the kinds of children in our group are children with "Williams syndrome." They are very articulate, both orally and in writing, as well as very sociable, and they can understand complex sentences and correct grammatical mistakes, but they cannot add two numbers together, tie their shoes or cross a street alone.[5] How all these groups, and all the anecdotal and systematic evidence, fit together is a challenge which we can only hope to cope with in a preliminary way in the final chapter that follows.

five

Facts, Thoughts, and Questions

On the one hand, it might seem desirable to initiate therapy as early as possible to give the child the best opportunity of overcoming the impairment before starting school. On the other hand, the disorder might resolve naturally, and treatment could create more problems than it solves by producing low expectations in teachers, anxiety in parents, and self-consciousness in the child.

— D. V. M. BISHOP AND A. EDMUNDSON[1]

No one knows exactly why children talk late, nor has anyone produced a formula to make them talk on schedule. However, there are some things that are known as a result of scientific research and some informed opinions on the part of those familiar with that research. In addition, I would like to offer a layman's thoughts, based partly on what I have learned from specialists and partly on what I have learned from our own group of late-talking children. My hope is that some of this will prove to be useful to parents and to those who come in contact with children like ours in schools or medical facilities. Perhaps most important of all, my hope is that specialists will take an interest in the patterns of bright children who talk late and use their expertise to carry the research further. Our detailed data will be made available to anyone who wishes to do such research.

What the patterns of the children in our group and children with Williams Syndrome suggest is that there is no such unitary thing as "intelligence," for these patterns show that it is possible for an individual to have levels of analytical ability far beyond the normal for children of the same age, while at the same time being unable to speak a simple sentence—and, conversely, that it is also possible to be highly articulate and yet be incapable of the simplest arithmetic. Some even more remarkable mental performances of autistic children support the same conclusion. Both the abilities and the disabilities in all three groups go beyond any range of variations that might plausibly be attributed to child-rearing practices. Specialists have in fact traced a gene which is believed to act on the brains of those with Williams Syndrome in such a way as to impair a particular kind of thinking, while leaving some other kinds of thinking and verbalizing abilities intact.[2]

Many late-talking children do not have a permanent impairment but only a delay that is eventually overcome. But it is at least worth considering whether this too might be biological rather than environmental in origin. The distinctive patterns of both the children in our group, and of the families from which they come, suggest some hereditary cause for their talking late.

At one time, it was common to blame parents, and especially mothers, when children failed to develop in the usual or expected way. Some of the parents in our group report being told by relatives and friends that they have been too eager to anticipate and respond to their child's needs, relieving him of the necessity or the incentive to learn to communicate. But the evidence against this explanation is too varied and too strong.

First of all, if the children talked late because of the parents' child-rearing practices, the most obvious question is: Why did their brothers and sisters not talk late then, when raised by the same parents? In most of those 36 families in our group where there were siblings, the sibling did not talk late—and in one of the families where they did, these were identical twins, who would be expected to be the same in many things. Nor does the explanation seem likely that the parents were over-anxious about the firstborn and then learned to wait and let the later children ask for what they wanted. More of the children in our group are the youngest than are the oldest. Why would the parents have reared the previous children "right" and then reared the last one "wrong"? Some are middle children, which would mean that the parents' child-rearing practices would have had to change back and forth, if that were the explanation for the late talking.

Perhaps most important of all, child-rearing practices would not explain why these children's close relatives included so many people in highly analytical occupations and/or with musical skills. Nor would it explain why these children themselves so often display unusual analytical abilities and why some of those who were given musical instruments seem to have taken to them so readily. Moreover, specialists who have studied other late-talking children have not attributed speech delay to child-rearing practices and some specialists have also warned against trying to "make" the child talk when he is not yet ready, as this can cause other problems.[3]

If an understanding of why some children talk late—and, for our particular group, why a distinctive pattern of abilities accompanies the speech delay—lies in heredity, then we are talking about something within the child himself. The most plausible place to look is where the power of speech itself originates, in the brain. By speech is not meant simply the physical control of the mouth and vocal chords in producing sound. What is meant is the whole *intellectual* process by which language is formulated before it is spoken—a process engaged in by deaf-mutes using sign language, as well as by others using vocal speech.[4]

THE BRAIN

Ideally, we would like an explanation not only concerning the central fact that our group of children talk late, but also concerning the associated phenomena—the overwhelmingly male group, the families with analytical and musical talents, and the late toilet training. Moreover, we would like to know what to do about the late talking, if anything can be done. Definitive answers to these questions cannot be provided here. The most we can hope for right now is to begin groping in the right direction. We can begin with what is known by people who have studied the brain.

A number of scientific studies have located where most people's speech is controlled, in a particular region of the brain's left hemisphere.[5] Other things located in the left hemisphere include analytical faculties. A study of musicians with perfect pitch likewise found, by magnetic resonance imaging, that the region of the left hemisphere where that ability is located was about 40 percent larger than the corresponding region of their right hemisphere, an asymmetry significantly greater than among other musicians or among the general public.[6]

Some other aspects of the brain may also be relevant to the situation of the children in our group. The brain controls more than intellectual activities or emotional states. It also controls both conscious and unconscious physical activities, including the operation of the immune system. Research on high-IQ individuals has found that such individuals tend to have much higher incidences of allergies and other immune system disorders, as well as a much higher incidence of left-handedness, than that of the general population.[7] A sample of very intellectually precocious children studied at Johns Hopkins University showed that four-fifths were myopic and/or allergic and/or left-handed.[8]

While about 10 percent of the general population suffer from allergies, more than half the students in the special program for intellectually precocious youngsters at John Hopkins had allergies. A survey at a meeting of Mensa, the international society for people with very high IQs, showed that 31 percent of those present reported "severe or multiple allergies."[9] Myopia is also more common among people with high intellectual abilities. While about 20 percent of normal children of the same age as those in the Johns Hopkins group had myopia, 53 percent of the mathematically precocious students had myopia, as did 75 percent of those who were verbally precocious and 72 percent of those who were precocious in both areas.[10] Other studies have likewise shown high-IQ individuals to be more likely to have myopia.[11] The incidence of left-handedness is higher than normal among mathematicians, architects, and astronauts.[12] These physical anomalies are all the more striking because high-IQ people tend in general to be physically healthier than average.[13] Why then, these particular physical anomalies?

Before trying to address that question, it is worth noting also that there are sex differences in the brain and, more specifically, in the way the brain operates when speaking.[14] Conceivably, this might have something to do with the fact that few girls have the distinctive combination of problems and abilities found among the late-talking children in our group. The chemistry of the brain is of course also different between the sexes because they have different combinations of hormones. Published research indicates that male hormones promote the kinds of brain functions involved in abstract spatial conceptions and mathematics.[15] This is also consistent with test results in which males outnumber females by 13 to 1 among those rare junior high school students who can score 700 or higher on the mathematics portion of the Scholastic Aptitude Test.[16]

In the light of this, it is hardly surprising that our group of late-talking children with special analytical abilities is overwhelmingly male. There are other factors as well, however.

The brains of females usually operate somewhat differently from the brains of most males in not having their thinking about particular things so confined to one region.[17] Finally, it is known that, in early childhood, brain cells are not as specialized as they will become later on, so that a given cell might be taken over to perform one function or a different function as the brain evolves. Another way of saying the same thing is that there is a competition for brain cells in early childhood among the various functions performed by the brain.

What do all these miscellaneous facts about the brain mean? One authority on the brain points out that extraordinarily gifted people "make considerable demands on the cell networks most involved in carrying out those tasks at which they excel"—possibly to the detriment of other functions performed by the brain. Thus humans have less sense of smell than animals and high IQ humans have more myopia, since both the olfactory and the optical functions make large demands of their own on the brain's resources.[18] Myopia among bright youngsters has sometimes been popularly attributed to their greater amount of reading but the same authority says, "childhood myopia is primarily, if not exclusively, a hereditary condition."[19]

Other functions—both intellectual and non-intellectual—which are carried on in the brain might likewise suffer from the demands made by other parts of the brain. Among the jeopardized functions are the immune system and control of the right hand by the left hemisphere, for example. Applying the same reasoning used to suggest that the sense of smell and the sense of sight may be adversely affected by unusual intellectual demands on the resources of the brain would offer a possible explanation for the higher incidence of allergies and other immune disorders, and of left-handedness, among people with high levels of analytical abilities.

What if the development of speech, which has large demands of its own to make on the resources of the brain, is also adversely affected by the competing demands of unusual analytical abilities? That would be consistent not only with the later development of speech in children like many of those in our group, it would also be consistent with this pattern's being much more common among boys than among girls. As already noted, the female brain not only operates differently during speech, but also does not have its functions as localized as among males. If sufficient brain resources for speech—whether cells, connecting networks or nutrients— are not available in one locality, the female brain may be more able to perform that same function somewhere else, as it performs other functions at more locations than in the male brain.

When Einstein's brain was examined after his death, it was found to be no heavier than average, but to have one portion of the left hemisphere that was twice the normal size.[20] Whether the resource demands of that enlarged sector of his brain contributed to his talking late is of course unknowable. But the possibility that this is so as a general phenomenon may be well worth exploring by people with the expertise to do so.

We have tended to describe the children in our group as youngsters who talk late despite being very bright in many cases. It is possible, however, that they are talking late precisely because they are very bright in a particular set of functions. Although bright children in general do not talk late, and often talk early,[21] our children's brightness is concentrated in a particular slice of the intellectual spectrum, based on abilities known to be localized in the left half of the brain. Our children seem more like engineers than like poets, more likely to master the computer than to master political intrigue.

If the explanation for the late speech development of children such as those in our group lies in this direction, that might help explain why their families contain so many people with similar abilities. But it would not explain why their brothers and sisters do not talk late. However, the normal statistical variation represented by a bell curve might account for that. Given a family whose combinations of hereditary abilities—whose brains—differ from the norm, a more extreme case of that deviation could put an individual in a range where the demands of unusually keen analytical functions may be met at the expense of other functions, such as speech.

The remarkable functioning of one of the brain's abilities might of course also—or instead—be at the expense of a different function, such as the immune system. If something has to give, that something may not be the same for all. This might help explain why our late-talking children, unlike other individuals with similarly unusual analytical abilities, tend to be overwhelmingly right-handed (94 percent), and to have no unusually high incidence of allergies. Perhaps the sacrifice of speech has made it unnecessary to sacrifice other things, at least not to the same extent as among some other children.

Research has shown that localized damage to a particular region of the brain is much more likely to permanently impair the related function in a boy than in a girl, whose brain could perform the same function somewhere else. By the same token, localized deprivation of resources in the brain might be expected to delay the development of the related function—speech in this case—more so for young boys than for young girls. All generalizations of course have exceptions, so that some girls may have speech delays for the same reasons as boys, even if this is rarer in females. The girls in our group seem to be like the boys in both their abilities and their family backgrounds.

To complete this line of reasoning, autistic children are in some ways more extreme examples of the set of abilities and disabilities found in our group. Indeed, some members of our group have been diagnosed as autistic, though the diagnosis itself has usually been retracted later, as the child's development unfolds. In one case, this diagnosis was retracted just 45 minutes later, when the doctor's first impression was abandoned after examination of the child. Another suggestive fact about autism is that it has been found to be six times as prevalent in the families of members of Mensa as in the general population.[22] In the case of Trevor Tao, two of his brothers won medals at the international mathematics Olympiads and one was working on his doctorate in mathematics at Princeton at the age of 19. Can autism too be a result of extraordinary hereditary abilities reaching the point where their demands on the brain's resources adversely affect other functions of the brain, or at least leave too thin a margin for coping with stresses that may arise? In cases where children have been known to outgrow autism, they have also been known to lose their unusual abilities, along with the negative features of autism.[23]

This still leaves no clue as to why toilet-training usually occurs somewhat later than usual among the late-talking children or why their social development seems slower than normal, or why so many of them seem so strong-willed. Here environmental factors may be at work, as parents may be less likely to press a child to conform when they are not sure of his understanding or ability to conform to social norms. However, brain factors need not be dismissed as possibilities, since people oriented toward left-hemisphere patterns may be less attuned to the emotional and social traits centered in the right hemisphere.

Research has also revealed that certain kinds of connections within the brain reach their peak in early childhood and decline thereafter—which is to say, the brain's ability to do certain kinds of things is greater in small children than in adults. Some specialists regard this as the reason why small children can master a foreign language more readily, more completely, and without accent, than an adult can.[24] Since any language is a foreign language at the beginning of life, this suggests that there is a certain window of opportunity for mastering language in general. Beyond some age, the evolving brain may never again be so capable of learning to speak or to understand words.

This raises a painful dilemma for the parents of late-talking children. They cannot afford to wait indefinitely, lest an opportunity be lost forever, but neither can they try to force the child to do something which his brain is not yet ready to do. Within our group, children who later grew up to lead normal lives have talked as late as 5 years of age, but of course such a generality cannot be applied in a blanket fashion to all children, and no parents have any way of knowing whether it will apply to their own child.

Here good professional advice could be invaluable, though it is by no means easy to find, as the experiences of some of the parents in our group show. Some professionals have been unbelievably hasty and dogmatic. In addition, those professionals working for the public school system have built-in incentives to label children and put them into special programs, which often get the school system more money from the government. Moreover, these programs need a steady supply of warm bodies, in order to keep going, whether or not they help or hurt the particular child.

My own inclination would be to get at least two private professional evaluations from people who are highly recommended and who are wholly independent of one another. Public schools often offer free evaluation services, but it would be penny-wise and pound-foolish to risk a wrong decision for a child, with lifelong consequences, in order to save the cost of independent examinations. As for private evaluations, a second *independent* opinion is a very worthwhile investment. The independence of that second opinion is crucial. A doctor who wants to know what the first doctor said before making his own assessment defeats much of the purpose of a second opinion. A doctor recommended by the first doctor may also not be the best investment of time and money. It may be more time-consuming to get two independently selected specialists at two separate institutions, preferably in different communities, but it can be time well consumed, given the high stakes.

TESTING

Both parents and testers need to be very clear as to just what it is that they are trying to find out. They are not trying to pinpoint an IQ but to determine whether the child does or does not have the potential to develop into an adult able to take care of himself. The question is whether he will or will not be dependent on others the rest of his life.

Medical tests may have a more or less focussed agenda, to try to determine whether hearing impairments, brain damage, or other physical problems are causing the child to have difficulty in speaking. Psychological testing, however, is often trying to determine more subtle or subjectively perceived influences—and how the child responds may depend on how the test situation itself is perceived on that given day. Where children have grown angry, tearful, frantic or violent after hours of psychological testing, the validity of evaluations made under these conditions is open to serious question. Moreover, it is not clear that all this is necessary, when the purpose is simply to discern whether or not a particular child has so little potential that he will never be able to take care of himself. Moreover, scholars who have studied late-talking children have found that, at age four, just one hour spent assessing such children's general prospects "correctly predicted in 90% of the children, and the few errors in prediction were not serious, insofar as they involved children who fell close to the borderline dividing good and bad outcome."[25]

For some of the children in our group, the evaluations themselves were traumas for all concerned—the children, the parents and the testers. One father wrote: "I believe Bryan is really beginning to hate these repeated examinations." Other parents admit that they hate these sessions as much as the child does. Words like "difficult," "impossible," and "*very* stressful" appear among the parents' characterizations of evaluation sessions. Too often, the professionals who conduct these evaluations end up with nothing useful to offer the parents except for some labels that tell them no more than they knew before—"delayed language development," for example—or which reach conclusions such as "autism" that are subsequently belied by the child's later development.

Those who conduct these evaluations have ranged from local school personnel to neurologists. Too often, those who are most certain are those with the least qualifications, including teachers, day care center directors, speech therapists and relatives. Those parents who sought second opinions from more highly qualified professionals often received a very different evaluation. However, even highly qualified professionals can turn out to be wrong, as two indicated to me, years after they had formed a more negative opinion of my son's prospects than his later development showed.

Quite aside from the conclusions reached as a result of evaluations, the evaluation process itself is in dire need of re-evaluation. The haste to label and the utter absence of common sense in dealing with small children are two of the biggest problems. One of the most common reasons for labelling is the illusion of having said something substantive by using a word or a phrase. Beyond this, however, there are professional, financial and even legal reasons to label.

Professionals are expected to deliver results—and they want to. The frustration of not being able to in the case of children who are maturing at their own pace and marching to their own drummer can promote labelling as one way of disposing of the embarrassment, especially when the child does not respond to approaches that work well with most other children. There is also the kind of professional self-interest revealed among those evaluating David from our group, who regarded him as a "gold mine" for their own research. Looking at children as potential guinea pigs also promotes labelling.

That anyone could have planned evaluation sessions that would go on for hours at a time with small children is surprising enough in itself, at least to anyone who has been a parent of a small child, whether "average" or not. That these sessions should continue on in bureaucratic fashion while the child is crying or trying to escape from the room is incredible. And to let evaluations done under such conditions produce labels that can change the course of a child's life is truly staggering.

A professional psychologist with whom I discussed this—a woman with the rare combination of a Ph.D. and common sense—was disgusted but not surprised when I told her of the hours-long evaluation sessions to which some of these children had been subjected. Since large elements of personal judgment are required, both for conducting the evaluation and for reaching conclusions, everything depends on the quality of the particular individuals involved. My friend's assessment was that the quality of people used by school districts was often not up to the task.

More is involved here than simple inadequacy, however. To change routines to take into account what is happening before your eyes may be only common sense and common decency, but it means taking personal responsibility—and few bureaucrats are willing to do that. Following the prescribed procedures, though the skies may fall, is the path of professional safety and the path of least resistance. Even if your conclusions prove to be miles off target, you can take refuge in having done everything "by the book." That may be important not only in terms of protecting one's career, but also in protecting oneself against lawsuits.

Then there are the experts specializing in autism. They are in one sense particularly well qualified for saying whether a given child does or does not fit this category. On the other hand, to some of these experts "autism" is just a label to be used for the sake of expediency in getting government funding of help that the child needs on other grounds. Others are engaged in a campaign to downgrade the shock of the term by applying it widely. Still others may simply have a specialist's bias, expressed by one of the parents in our group as: "To a hammer, everything looks like a nail."

Even mental tests that are fine in themselves may have to be used and interpreted with great care. Perhaps the worst example of failing to do this with some of the children in our group involved an IQ test administered to a boy who was legally blind, with those questions requiring better eyesight than he had being marked wrong. The resulting IQ of 70 had no relationship to his actual mental ability, as different tests later showed. No test, however valid in itself, is immune to mindless misuse.

It would be a major humanitarian service to late-talking children and their parents to institute shorter evaluation procedures, which can assess the child without causing such an emotional breakdown that the validity of the results themselves are jeopardized. If, as scholars who have specialized in this subject have said, a *one-hour* assessment of late-talking children at age four has a high degree of predictive validity, then the question must be raised whether longer and more questionable procedures serve any purpose in most cases, other than allowing the evaluators to cover themselves. Medical examinations are of course another story, but often the longer procedures are used by school psychologists and other non-medical staff.

INSTITUTIONS

Many of the greatest difficulties in the lives of the children in our group are encountered in institutions—whether in day care centers, preschools, kindergartens, or in regular school systems. It is by no means always clear that these children are better off, on net balance, for having to be fitted into institutional routines, with the rigidities these often involve, before the children are talking and often before they have matured as much as other children. In many cases, there appears to be no serious problem in coping with the children at home. Only one of the 44 parents cited the day-to-day problems created by the child's delayed speech as the principal reason for their concern about that delay. Many parents did not cite it as a factor at all.

Where economic pressures leave no realistic alternative to having the child institutionalized at least part of each working day, so that both parents can have jobs, that is one thing. But those who do have feasible alternatives might well reconsider why an institutional setting is the place for a child with special needs. I certainly know that I regret that my son was put in a nursery school, where he retrogressed in more ways than one. From my own experience as a child, although I was not late in talking, I am in retrospect glad that I was never put into any institutional setting until I entered the public schools—which I did at age seven, because a succession of childhood diseases kept me home at age six. Boys are particularly likely to need more time to mature and boys are the great majority of late-talking children, not only in our group but elsewhere.

Why have needless struggles to get a young child to sit quietly in circles at school or otherwise conform to an institutional strait-jacket? What is so important about sitting in circles, except that it is one of the many fetishes of the education establishment? There have undoubtedly been many fine people in this world, including some truly great people, who have lived and died without ever having sat in a circle, and who were none the worse for missing this activity or inactivity. The child will encounter this kind of stuff all too soon when he is old enough to go to the public schools. Why needlessly impose it on him when he may not yet have the maturity to handle it—and when he has other problems to cope with? Nor is this necessarily a transient problem. The negative emotions and attitudes it can spawn—toward school, toward parents and toward the world—may long outlast the immediate problem and long outlast his late talking.

Much of the anguish of parents has also originated in institutions, with their hasty labels and narrow norms as to what constitutes learning or even social interaction. Children who are not learning in the particular way that has been designed have been treated as if they were not learning at all, even when they were doing things that most children their age could not do, just as the rather intense interaction between little Billy and Heidi in preschool was seen by a teacher there as "not interacting" because it did not fit some stereotype of what interaction should be.

The lockstep norms and progressions of educational and child-care institutions seem particularly likely to create needless problems for a child whose development is unfolding in a different pattern or at a different pace in some areas. The daily schedules that require everyone to change from one activity to another at the same time, regardless of individual interests, may be an institutional convenience or necessity, but that is wholly different from saying that a particular child is better off being subjected to such requirements at an early age. The same is true of the longer-run progression from one grade to another in lockstep with other children of the same chronological age. The wise decision of Kevin's mother to have him repeat kindergarten, when he was at the age prescribed for going into the first grade, paid off handsomely. But how many mothers would have had the fortitude to make such a request and how many school systems would have had the flexibility to allow it?

The fact that we all must, at some time or other, conform to institutional requirements is no reason to do so sooner, rather than later, especially for those families fortunate enough to have other options. Even where there is no feasible alternative but to have the child introduced to institutions at an early age, choices may still be made among institutions, not simply on the basis of their general reputations, but more specifically on their degree of individual flexibility in activities and schedules.

CONCLUSIONS AND QUESTIONS

What can parents of late-talking children do?

First of all, they can recognize that there are many children who talk late and very different reasons why they do. At least one subset of such children is not merely "normal" in intelligence, but often well above normal in some respects, as some of the children in our group obviously are. Whether a given child is simply delayed in speaking or has serious mental or other disabilities is a crucial question, for which good professional evaluation is essential.

The kinds of children who talk late but then go on to do well in schools and colleges, and to have careers in demanding fields, may be more common than I would have suspected just a year or two ago. My discussions of our group with colleagues and friends has often brought forth more examples and some parents in the group report having similar experiences. There seem to be a lot of such people out there, who are only mentioned when this particular subject is brought up. Yet there has been no systematic information on these people before, nor even much awareness of their existence.

Where late-talking is a transient phenomenon, it is almost as if it never happened, as far as the experiences of people outside the family are concerned. In adulthood, the individual himself is often unaware that he talked late—something which usually had nothing like the ominous meaning and emotional stress for the child that it did for the parent—and may discover delayed speech in his past only if and when the parent has an occasion to mention it. The result is that each new parent with a bright child who talks late is likely to feel as baffled and isolated as those who went before, simply because of being unaware of those who went before, even if they live in the same neighborhood. Nor are many professional specialists likely to accumulate a large store of information or experience about the continuing development of such children, since parents are likely to stop taking their children to see these specialists after they begin talking.

The experiences of the parents and children in our group may help fill some of the void, both for parents and for those who come in contact with bright, late-talking children in schools and other settings. If nothing else, these experiences should promote caution among those who might otherwise be quick to label a child, risking needless anguish for the parents and long-run damage to the child, especially if he gets swallowed up by one of the many special programs from which few emerge into a normal school setting. Parents must also be prepared to fight for their children's interests and not be manipulated or intimidated by the education system's "experts" and smooth talkers. If you need a real expert, hire your own.

If competent medical authorities discover some recognizable reason for the child's delay in talking, then they are likely also to be the best source of advice on what to do about it. But what if medical science ends up as baffled as the parents, because specialists can find nothing wrong and the child seems obviously bright? There are no miracle methods for getting the child talking, but patience, love, and attention may be the best help for this, as for many other things. Research has shown that interaction with adults helps a child's mental development, even if the adults themselves are low-IQ individuals. Apparently the brain itself is permanently better off for this early childhood stimulation.[26] In other words, neither advanced people nor advanced gadgets are necessary to promote a small child's mental development.

Most of the parents in our group took their child to a speech therapist but not all were convinced that this did much good. Much may depend on the age and stage of development at which speech therapy begins. If the child is simply not yet ready for speech, then attempts to force it may be counterproductive, as well as risking devastating diagnoses from a frustrated therapist who may have no qualifications for making any diagnosis at all. However, once the child is beginning to talk, then therapy may be very effective, as it was for my son and for others in our group. So may reading to the child, tape-recording his words and playing them back, or other methods that may occur to parents. If the hypothesis that speech delay among bright children reflects a later development of that part of the brain where speech originates is correct, then attempts to force speech seem especially ill-advised.

This survey should be only the beginning of efforts to understand this particular subset of late-talking children and their special abilities and distinctive family backgrounds. These children's development needs to be followed over a period of years and perhaps decades. Some of the questions asked in the survey—about allergies or ear infections, for example—were not intended to tell us much immediately, but rather to allow follow-up research to determine if those with particular sets of characteristics turned out differently from others and what that implies for the diagnoses of other such children in the future.

Since I am past the age at which it makes sense to begin following people for decades, I would particularly welcome any interest by medical or scientific specialists in taking our data and carrying the research forward. In the meantime, perhaps what parents of late-talking children need to know above all is: You are not alone. Those of us in our group have been there before you, and some are still there, struggling with present problems and future uncertainties. Although late-talking in general has often been a sign of other serious and lasting problems, many parents of intelligent children who talk late have found light at the end of the tunnel—sometimes very bright light.

Notes

CHAPTER THREE: PATTERNS IN THE GROUP

1. Marilyn Solomon, "Speechless at 3, Top Grad Has Final Word," *Nashua Telegraph*, June 25, 1994, p. 16

CHAPTER FOUR: PATTERNS OUTSIDE THE GROUP

1. D. V. M. Bishop and A. Edmundson, "Language-Impaired 4-Year-Olds: Distinguishing Transient from Persistent Impairment," *Journal of Speech and Hearing Disorders*, Vol. 52, No. 2 (May 1987), p. 166.

2. Phil A. Silva, Rob McGee and Sheila M. Williams, "Developmental Language Delay from Three to Seven Years and Its Significance for Low Intelligence and Reading Difficulties at Age Seven," *Development Medicine and Child Neurology*, Vol. 25, No. 6 (December 1983), p. 783.

3. Kenneth M. McRae and Eric Vickar, "Simple Developmental Speech Delay: A Follow-Up Study," *Developmental Medicine and Child Neurology*, Vol. 33, No. 10 (1991), pp. 868–874,

4. Kenneth M. McRae and Eric Vickar, "Simple Developmental Speech Delay: A Follow-Up Study," *Developmental Medicine and Child Neurology*, Vol. 33, No. 10 (1991), p. 868.

5. Steven Pinker, *The Language Instinct: How the Mind Creates Language* (New York: William Morrow, 1994), pp. 52–53;

CHAPTER FIVE: FACTS, THOUGHTS, AND QUESTIONS

1. D. V. M. Bishop and A. Edmundson, "Language-Impaired 4-Year-Olds: Distinguishing Transient from Persistent Impairment," *Journal of Speech and Hearing Disorders*, Vol. 52, No. 2 (May 1987), pp. 156–173.

2. Steven Pinker, *The Language Instinct: How the Mind Creates Language* (New York: William Morrow, 1994), p. 52.

3. Kenneth M. McRae and Eric Vickar, "Simple Developmental Speech Delay: A Follow-Up Study," *Developmental Medicine and Child Neurology*, Vol. 33, No. 10 (1991), p. 872.

4. Steven Pinker, *The Language Instinct*, p. 302.

5. Miles G. Storfer, *Intelligence and Giftedness: The Contribution of Heredity and Early Environment* (San Francisco: Jossey-Bass, 1990), p. 345; Steven Pinker, *The Language Instinct: How the Mind Creates Language* (New York: William Morrow, 1994), p. 306. A cautionary note, however, is sounded by Elizabeth Bates, "Comprehension and Production in Early Language Development," *Monograph of the Society for Research in Child Development*, Vol. 58, Nos. 3–4 (1993), p. 239.

6. Paul Recer, "Brain's Left Side Has Perfect Pitch," *San Francisco Chronicle*, February 3, 1995, p. A7. For the original paper see Gottfried Schlaug, et al, "In Vivo Evidence of Structural Brain Asymmetry in Musicians," *Science*, Vol. 267 (3 February 1995), pp. 699–701.

7. Miles D. Storfer, *Intelligence and Giftedness*, pp. 383–394.

8. *Ibid.*, p. 385.

9. Miles G. Storfer, *Intelligence and Giftedness: The Contribution of Heredity and Early Environment* (San Francisco: Jossey-Bass, 1990), pp. 386, 389.

10. Miles G. Storfer, *Intelligence and Giftedness: The Contribution of Heredity and Early Environment* (San Francisco: Jossey-Bass, 1990), p. 385.

11. Camilia Persson Benbow, "Possible Biological Correlates of Precocious Mathematical Reasoning Ability," *Trends in Neurosciences*, Vol. 10 (January 1987), p. 18.

12. Camilla Persson Benbow, "Possible Biological Correlates of Precocious Mathematical Reasoning Ability, *Trends in Neurosciences*, Vol. 10 (January 1987), p. 18.

13. This was found to be true in the most famous group of high-IQ people, those followed over a lifetime by Lewis M. Terman. Joel N. Shurkin, *Terman's Kids: The Groundbreaking Study of How the Gifted Grow Up* (Boston: Little, Brown, 1992), p. 45.

14. Gina Kolata, "Men and Women Use Brain Differently, Study Discovers," *New York Times*, February 16, 1995, p. A 1; Bennett A.

Shaywitz, et al, "Sex Differences in the Functional Organization of the Brain for Language," *Nature*, Vol. 373 (16 February 1995), pp. 607–609.

15. Daniel B. Hier, M. D., and William F. Crowley, M.D., "Spatial Ability in Androgen-Deficient Men," *The New England Journal of Medicine*, May 20, 1982, pp. 1202–1205. See also Jerome Kagan, "The Idea of Spatial Ability," *Ibid.*, pp. 1225–1226; Sandra Blakeslee, "Man's Test Scores Linked to Hormones," *New York Times*, November 14, 1991, p. A 11; Camilla Persson Benbow and Robert M. Benbow, "Biological Correlates of High Mathematical Reasoning Ability," *Progress in Brain Research*, Vol. 61 (1984), pp. 469–490.

16. Miles D. Storfer, *Intelligence and Giftedness*, p. 363.

17. Christine Gorman, "How Gender May Bend Your Thinking," *Time*, July 17, 1996, p. 51; Bennett A. Shavitz, et al, "Sex Differences in the Functional Organization of the Brain for Language," *Nature*, 16 February 1995, pp. 607–609.

18. Miles G. Storfer, *Intelligence and Giftedness: The Contribution of Heredity and Early Environment* (San Francisco: Jossey-Bass, 1990), pp. 391–393.

19. Miles G. Storfer, *Intelligence and Giftedness: The Contribution of Heredity and Early Environment* (San Francisco: Jossey-Bass, 1990), p. 385.

20. Miles G. Storfer, *Intelligence and Giftedness: The Contribution of Heredity and Early Environment* (San Francisco: Jossey-Bass, 1990), pp. 390, 393.

21. The high-IQ youngsters in Lewis Terman's famous longitudinal study began talking, on average, about three and a half months earlier than normal. However, four boys and one girl were two years old or older when they began talking and one boy in another group of high-IQ students began talking somewhere between age three and three and a half. Lewis M. Terman, *Genetic Studies of Genius*, Volume I: *Mental and Physical Traits of a Thousand Gifted Children* (Stanford: Stanford University Press, 1925), pp. 186, 573; Lewis M. Terman and Melita H. Oden, *The Gifted Group at Mid-Life: Thirty-Five Years' Follow-Up of the Superior Child* (Stanford: Stanford University Press, 1967), p. 7.

22. Miles G. Storfer, *Intelligence and Giftedness: The Contribution of Heredity and Early Environment* (San Francisco: Jossey-Bass, 1990),

p. 390. Reinforcing this pattern is the comment of a man with many years of research on autistic children, "children with symptoms of classical early infantile autism are almost invariably the offspring of parents of exceptional intelligence, which suggests their abilities may be inherited." Bernard Rimland, "Inside the Mind of the Autistic Savant," *Psychology Today*, August 1978, p. 80

23. Bernard Rimland, "Inside the Mind of the Autistic Savant," *Psychology Today*, August 1978, p. 70.

24. Steven Pinker, *The Language Instinct: How the Mind Creates Language* (New York: William Morrow, 1994), pp. 293–296.

25. D. V. M. Bishop and A. Edmundson, "Language-Impaired 4-Year-Olds: Distinguishing Transient from Persistent Impairment," *Journal of Speech and Hearing Disorders*, Vol. 52, No. 2 (May 1987).

26. Michele Block Morse, "Brain Power: New Evidence Confirms that Early Stimulation Makes a Big Difference Later On," *Parents Magazine*, Vol. 69, No. 9 (September 1994), pp. 61–62.

APPENDIX:

SURVEYS, RESULTS, AND FUTURE SURVEYS

Introduction

This survey was meant to be the first word, not the last, on bright children who talk late. Future surveys can benefit from my mistakes, as well as from the information already gained. To facilitate both benefits, this Appendix contains copies of the questionnaires sent out in the 1994 and 1996 surveys. It also contains a tabulation of the results of the second survey, which encompasses virtually everything that was in the first survey and does so for a larger sample. Those who wish to get the data in computerized form, which they can tabulate and break down in their own ways, can do so by simply writing to me at the Hoover Institution, Stanford, California 94305. Those who are interested in doing follow-up studies or otherwise studying this group more deeply can write to me at the same address. I have no proprietary interests in this work and I am at an age where follow-up studies in later years should be done by someone younger. Nor do I have any vested interest in being proved right in my assessments or speculations. It is infinitely more important to find out whatever we can about the truth, whatever that truth may turn out to be.

In view of a surprising lack of IQ data for the children in our group, one of the things a follow-up study should do is to determine their IQ scores or other standardized test scores. Because of the increased incidence of allergies and left-handedness among high-IQ individuals in general, a follow-up study should determine whether those children in our group who have many or severe allergies later turn out differently—whether in talking, on IQ tests, or by other measures of success—from those with few or mild allergies, and whether those who are left-handed turn out differently from those who are right-handed. Follow-up studies can also determine whether the mental test results of the children in this group during the early years of life correlate with either their later development of speech or with the scores on mental tests given after their language skills have matured.

It is very important to determine which assessment methods offer the most reliable predictions of the future development of late-talking children, whether these methods be medical examinations, mental testing or something else. It is particularly important to determine how many of the diagnoses of autism or of other syndromes held up over the years and how far they diverged from reality when they did not.

The logistics of arranging follow-up studies of the children in our group will depend, among other things, on whether I am still around at the time or on whatever arrangements my successors will make. My primary requirement is that whatever research is done protect the privacy of the families involved and live up to the pledges of confidentiality that they have asked for and have been given on the questionnaires. My successors should feel bound by the same pledges, whether or not they are as personally acquainted as I am with the ruthlessness of some media people when they are pursuing a story. The last thing a family with a late-talking child needs is to find a television sound truck parked outside their home or to have the adults or the children in the family pursued by reporters.

One way of doing follow-up studies of the children in this group without compromising their privacy would be for a later survey to be done within our group, by me or a successor, and then put on computer disks with the same individuals being identified from one survey to the next by their respective birthdates. If some reputable medical or scientific organization wished to take over the whole project, including the folders containing the letters, photos and other materials sent to me, I would be willing to consider that very seriously—with the approval of the parents concerned. Other arrangements are also possible.

For the benefit of whoever might do a follow-up study, the deficiencies of this first survey need to be noted, so that the next one can be better. But first we should look at the questionnaires used, before critiquing them.

First Questionnaire (1994)

QUESTIONNAIRE FOR PARENTS OF LATE-TALKING CHILDREN

CHILD'S NAME	DATE OF BIRTH								
AGE WHEN FIRST WORD WAS SPOKEN									
AGE WHEN FIRST STATEMENT WAS MADE USING MORE THAN ONE WORD									
AGE WHEN THE CHILD FIRST SPOKE IN COMPLETE SENTENCES									
AGE WHEN BACK-AND-FORTH CONVERSATION FIRST OCCURRED									
WAS THE CHILD TESTED FOR MENTAL ABILITY? AT WHAT AGE OR AGES?									
WHAT KIND OF TEST OR TESTS?									
WHAT RESULTS?									
THINGS IN WHICH THE CHILD'S ABILITY APPEARS TO BE AHEAD OF OTHERS HIS AGE									
THINGS IN WHICH THE CHILD'S ABILITY APPEARS TO BE BEHIND OTHERS HIS AGE									
THINGS IN WHICH THE CHILD'S ABILITY APPEARS TO BE ABOUT THE SAME AS THAT OF OTHERS HIS AGE									

WHAT IS THE CHILD'S MEMORY LIKE?

THE CHILD'S SPECIAL INTERESTS

THINGS DISLIKED BY THE CHILD

HAVE YOU TRIED A SPEECH THERAPIST? IF SO, AT WHAT AGE AND WITH WHAT RESULT?

HAVE YOU HAD SPECIALISTS EVALUATE YOUR SON? IF SO, AT WHAT AGE AND WITH WHAT RESULT? WAS THE EXAMINATION ITSELF A DIFFICULT EXPERIENCE FOR HIM?

AT WHAT AGE DID HE BEGIN TO USE THE POTTY OR TOILET FOR URINATION? FOR BOWEL MOVEMENTS?

MATHEMATICALLY-RELATED OCCUPATIONS OR EDUCATION BY FAMILY MEMBERS, WHETHER CURRENTLY OR NOT

(include grandparents, uncles, aunts, etc., in such fields as science, engineering, medicine, computers, economics, statistics, etc.)

MUSICALLY-RELATED OCCUPATION OR EDUCATION BY FAMILY MEMBERS AT ANY TIME

ADDITIONAL INFORMATION OR EXPLANATIONS

(Add more pages if you need more space)

Do not mention my name or the name of my child in print.

You may mention our first names in print and the initial of our family name.

Do not mention the community in which we live.

SIGNATURE:_____

NAME PRINTED: _____

SECOND QUESTIONNAIRE (1996)

QUESTIONNAIRE FOR STUDY OF LATE-TALKING CHILDREN

I. EARLY CHILDHOOD

1. At what age did you become seriously concerned because your child was not talking? _____

2. Why was the child's late talking considered to be a problem *at that time*? (Check box below. If more than one reason, put a 1 in the box of the most important reason, 2 in the box for the next most important, etc.)

    The child was unhappy at not being able to communicate. ☐

    Parents were unhappy with the day to day problems caused by the child's not talking. ☐

    The normal time for the child to talk had come and gone, causing concern for the child's future. ☐

    Other (write below and/or on back of page): ☐

3. Check which of the following apply to your child:

    Left-handed ☐   Right-handed ☐   Ambidextrous ☐

    Many or severe allergies ☐   Few or mild allergies ☐   Practically no allergies ☐

Many or severe
ear infections

Few or mild
ear infections

Practically
no ear infections

Clumsy for his
or her age

Average in
physical skills

Above average in
physical skills

Unusually good at
puzzles, such as
putting cut-out shapes
into a board.

About average
at such things
for children of
the same age

Below
average
at such
puzzles

Ability at such puzzles
never tested or noticed

Child fascinated by:

water (in tubs or streams,
pools, lakes, etc.)

spinning objects

Other

If "other," please specify:

No special fascinations

4. Did the child in early childhood prefer toys aimed at girls, such as dolls, or toys aimed at boys, such as toy trucks or trains, or was there no difference in his or her preferences?

    Generally preferred   Generally preferred   No preference
    toys for girls   toys for boys

    [ ]   [ ]   [ ]

5. Were playmates of one sex preferred to the other in settings where both were available?

        Preferred to play with girls   [ ]

        Preferred to play with boys   [ ]

        No particular preference either way   [ ]

        Only boys usually available   [ ]

        Only girls usually available   [ ]

II. FAMILY BACKGROUND

1. Child's place in the family:

        Only child   First born   Youngest   Adopted

        [ ]   [ ]   [ ]   [ ]

        Other (please specify):

        Number of sisters:

        Number of brothers:

Is there a sibling or other close relative who talked late?_____

Are there significantly more boys than girls, or vice versa, among your relatives?

2. Family educational and occupational background

Parent's education:

Level_____(diploma or degree)

Specialization_____ (field)

Parents' Occupations

    Mother:_____

    Father:_____

Family occupational backgrounds:
(please put a number in each cell to indicate how many family members in each category have worked in the occupation in question)

	Accountants	Computer specialists	Engineers	Mathematicians	Physicians	Pilots	Scientists	Other analytical (please specify)
Father								
Mother								
Grandfathers								
Grandmothers								
Aunts								
Uncles								

Please write an M in the appropriate box for each relative who plays or has played a musical instrument. Put an asterisk alongside the M for each one who played professionally or taught music.

3. Ethnic background:

	MOTHER	FATHER
European or White	☐	☐
African or Black	☐	☐
Chinese or Japanese	☐	☐
American Indian or Native American	☐	☐
India Indian	☐	☐
Other (please specify):	☐	☐

III. TALKING

1. Age when the child's first word was spoke:_____

2. Age when the child's first statement was made using more than one word:_____

3. Age when the child first spoke in complete sentences:_____

4. Age when back-and-forth conversation first occurred:_____

5. To what extent has the child's talking been accompanied by gestures, facial expressions, and/or body language coordinated with the words? Indicate by checking a box in the table below:

Much more so than most children the same age	Somewhat more so than most children the same age	Average for children the same age	Somewhat less than average for the age	Much less than average for the age

IV. SOCIAL DEVELOPMENT

How would you characterize the child's ability to handle social relations?

FAR BELOW AVERAGE	BELOW AVERAGE	AVERAGE	ABOVE AVERAGE	FAR ABOVE AVERAGE

V. MENTAL ABILITY

1. Indicate on the table below the age or ages at which your child's mental ability was tested, the name of the test, and the test scores or other index of his ability that resulted.

AGES	NAME OF TEST	SCORE OR OTHER INDICATOR
AGE:		
AGE:		
AGE:		
AGE:		

2. Please check one of the boxes below to indicate how you would characterize the child's memory.

Very poor	Below average	Average	Above average	Extremely good
☐	☐	☐	☐	☐

VI. MISCELLANEOUS

1. Evaluations

Have medical or psychological specialists examined your child as a result of his or her late talking?

YES ☐   NO ☐

Please indicate at what age these examinations took place, the profession of the person doing the examination (physician, psychologist, etc.), the process, and the results on the table below:

EXAMINATIONS	TITLES OF PERSONS EXAMINING THE CHILD	NAME OF TEST OR PROCEDURE	WAS THE PROCESS ITSELF STRESSFUL TO THE CHILD?	WHAT CONCLUSION WAS REACHED AFTER EXAMINATION?
CHILD'S AGE ON THE FIRST OCCASION				
CHILD'S AGE ON THE SECOND OCCASION				
CHILD'S AGE ON THE THIRD OCCASION				
CHILD'S AGE ON THE FOURTH OCCASION				

2. Child's Likes and Dislikes

Things especially liked by the child: _____

Things especially disliked by the child: _____

3. Have you had a speech therapist work with your child?

YES ☐   NO ☐

At what ages? _____

With what result? _____

4. At what age did the child become toilet-trained?

For urination: _____

For bowel movements: _____

VII. GROUP ACTIVITY:

Please check whichever statements below apply to you:

I have written letters to the group as a whole.	I have written individual members of the group without writing the group as a whole.	I have phoned other member(s) of the group.	I have been phoned by other member(s) of the group.	I have met other member(s) in person.
I always read letters and memos from the group.	I usually read letters and memos from the group.	I seldom read letters and memos from the group.	I never read letters and memos.	

PLEASE ADD ANY ADDITIONAL INFORMATION, EITHER FOR ITS OWN SAKE OR TO CLARIFY ANSWERS ALREADY GIVEN:

Information in this and previous questionnaire may be shown to physicians or other professionals doing research on this group, with your permission, as indicated by signing below. Family names will not be used in any publication nor will small communities be identified. If there are any other restrictions you wish, please indicate them before signing below:

NAME (printed) _____
SIGNATURE: _____

ADDRESS:

TELEPHONE NUMBER:

INSTRUCTIONS FOR TABULATING DATA FROM 1996 QUESTIONNAIRE

In order to facilitate interpretation of the data from the 1996 questionnaire, I include the instructions used for making those tabulations.

QUESTION	CLARIFICATION
Male/Female categories	This refers to the number of male and female individuals, not the number of families with a male or female child. Because there are two families with two late-talking children each, the number of individuals and the number of families will of course not coincide. More important, for most questions, the relevant answer is in terms of individuals, but for other (to be noted below) it is families.
Section I, Question 1	Since the age categories overlap, "1 to 1½ years" will mean between age one and age one and a half, so that a child who was exactly one and a half years old when his parents became concerned about his not talking would be recorded in the category "1½ to 2 years." The same principle applies to the other age categories as well. Moreover, because this is a question about parents, we do not wish to count the same parents twice where there is more than one late-talking child in the family, so the number that is relevant here is the number of families, not individuals.
Section I, Question 2	Since this is also a question about the parents, again the number here refers to the number of families, not individuals.
Section I, Question 3	Since this is a question about children, this number refers to individuals-- as do all other numbers not specifically designated as referring to families.
Section II, Question 1	This number should refer to families. Otherwise, not only will twins who talk late automatically count as two individuals with a relative who talked late, but each of their relatives who talked late will also be counted twice.

SECTION II, Question 2, "Occupations" table	The "occupations" table is a family table. That is, if two late-talking children in the same family have an uncle who is an accountant, that does not mean two accountants. This is a family table in another and more fundamental sense: What we ultimately want to know is what percentage of the families have an engineer, an accountant, etc., among the late-talking children's close relatives. That means that two uncles in one family who are accountants count as a *one* accountant in this table. Otherwise, if only one out of three families had an accountant among the children's close relatives, while that one family had three accountants, then the totals for the table would make it appear that 100 percent of the families had accountants, when only 33⅓ percent did. Therefore, no matter how many relatives might be listed on the questionnaires as being in a given occupation, enter just one for that occupation in that family. In this table, we are not counting the number of relatives who are accountants; we are counting the number of families where there is at least one relative who works in that occupation.
SECTION II, Question 1 "more boys than girls or vice-versa"	If there is not a sex imbalance on both sides of the family, this should be recorded as "no great difference." Where the answer on the questionnaire does not indicate whether it applies to the mother's relatives or the father's relatives, then assume that it applies to both and enter it accordingly.
SECTION II, Question 2	This is also a family table showing the number of families who have musicians among the close relatives of the late-talking children. If there is more than one musician per family, that does not change the number in the "yes" column but such families will also be counted (as one) in the "multiple" column. In other words, the same family can be counted in more than one column here.
SECTION II, Question 3	This is a family question, so that parents are not counted more than once when they have more than one child who talks late.
SECTIONS III, IV, V, and VI	All these are to be tabulated as individuals.
SECTION V, "Intelligence Quotient'	Where there are multiple scores, count the highest.
SECTION VI, Question 1	Count "pervasive development disorder" (PDD) as autism
SECTION VII	This is to be tabulated by family, to avoid counting the parents of multiple late-talkers more than once.

SURVEY RESULTS

SAMPLE SIZE:
    Individuals   46
    Families   44

I. EARLY CHILDHOOD:

1. Age at which parent became seriously concerned about child's inability to talk

Before age one	0
1 to 1½ years	4
1½ to 2 years	2
2 to 2½ years	17
2½ to 3 years	12
3 years +	11

2. Reason for concern about child's late talking:

Child's frustration	4
Daily problems	1
Behind schedule	31
Other	10

3. Children's general patterns:

Hand
Left-handed	2
Right-handed	43
Ambidextrous	1

Allergies
Many or severe	5
Few or mild	11
Practically none	30

Ear infections
Many or severe	15
Few or mild	8
Practically none	23

Physical skills
- Clumsy — 12
- Average — 18
- Above average — 16

Puzzles
- Unusually good — 31
- Average — 6
- Below average — 5
- Not noticed — 4

Fascinations
- Water — 19
- Spinning objects — 7
- Spinning self — 1
- Other — 23
- None — 14

4. Toys

Toys
- Preferred girl toys — 5
- Preferred boy toys — 25
- No preference — 16

5. Playmates

Preferences
- Preferred girls — 2
- Preferred boys — 4
- No preference — 37
- Only boys available — 1
- Only girls available — 3

II. FAMILY

1. Child's place in the family:

Child's place
- Only child — 9

First born   11
Youngest   19
Adopted   1
Other   6

Close relative who talked late?
yes   12
no   33

Relatives' children
More boys than girls   13
More girls than boys   6
No great difference   22

2. Family educational and occupational background:

Education

	MOTHER	FATHER
Less than high school	0	1
High school	2	2
Some college (includes associate degrees)	6	8
Finished college (4 yr.)	18	9
Postgraduate	9	15

Occupations of close relatives

OCCUPATIONS	NUMBER OF FAMILIES
Accountants	23
Computer specialists	15
Engineers	26
Mathematicians	2
Physicians	5
Pilots	6
Scientists	9
Other analytical	2 *

*both economists

Musicians among close relatives
Yes   35
No   7
Multiple   26
Professional   12

3. Race or ethnicity

	MOTHER	FATHER
White	40	38
Black	2	3
Chinese or Japanese	0	1
American Indian	0	1
India Indian	0	0
Other	1	0

III. Talking

AGE:	FIRST WORD	FIRST MULTI-WORD STATEMENT	FIRST SENTENCE	CONVERSATION
Before 1	6	0	0	0
1 to 1½	8	1	0	0
1½ to 2	5	3	0	0
2 to 2½	9	3	0	0
2½ to 3	6	6	1	0
3 to 3½	5	4	5	2
3½ to 4	2	7	5	7
4 to 4½	2	9	9	10
4½ to 5	0	2	7	4
5 +	1	3	10	14
Not yet	1	5	7	7

Integration of speech, gestures, and facial expressions

Much more so than most children the same age	12
Somewhat more so than most children the same age	6
Average for children the same age	11
Somewhat less than average for the age	8
Much less than average for the age	5

IV. Social development

	AS A CHILD	AS AN ADULT
Far below average	12	0
Below average	20	1
Average	6	1
Above average	7	3
Far above average	1	1

V. Mental ability

Intelligence quotient

	Non-verbal	Total
Below 90	1	1
from 90 to 110	2	3
Above 110	1	3

Other measures

	Non-verbal	Total
Below age level	0	4
Average for age level	1	3
Above average for age level	2	2

Parental assessment of child's memory

Memory	
Very poor	0
Below average	0
Average	0
Above average	19
Extremely good	27

VI. Miscellaneous

1. Evaluations

Evaluated by medical or psychological specialists?

yes	41
no	5

First evaluation
Process itself stressful to the child?

yes	20
no	16

Second evaluation
Process itself stressful to the child?

yes	9
no	17

Third evaluation
Process itself stressful to the child?
　　yes　　9
　　no　　　9

Evaluators' conclusions

　　autistic　　　　12
　　other disorder　12
　　no cause found　13

2. Child's likes and dislikes

	LIKES	DISLIKES
Music	10	0
Puzzles	8	1
Building things	6	0
Computers	13	0
New things	0	3
Noise	0	9

3. Speech therapist

Used speech therapist?
　　yes　　40
　　no　　　6
Age when therapist was used
　　By first birthday　　3
　　Age one　　　　　　0
　　Age two　　　　　　19
　　Age three　　　　　7
　　Age four　　　　　　7
　　Five or older　　　3

Results of speech therapy
　　Good　　　　22
　　Bad　　　　　1
　　None　　　　4
　　Doubtful　　10

4. Toilet training:

Age	Urination	Bowel movements
Before 1	0	0
1-1½	0	0
1½-2	2	2
2-2½	2	1
2½-3	4	3
3-3½	13	9
3½-4	6	8
4-4½	5	5
4½-5	5	4
5 +	4	8
Not yet	3	4

VII. GROUP ACTIVITY

Has written letters to the group	22
Has written letters to individuals	15
Has phoned other member(s)	14
Has been phoned by other member(s)	13
Has met other member(s) in person	3
Always read letters and memos	34
Usually read letters and memos	3
Seldom read letters and memos	1

SECOND THOUGHTS

SINCE HINDSIGHT IS 20/20, IT CAN HARDLY BE SURPRISING THAT there are many things I would do differently, after reflecting on the results. First of all, I would not have omitted the birthdates on the second questionnaire. Finding out those birthdates later took many phone calls, often more than one call to the same parents until I caught them at home or work. These dates, which did not seem so important while the questionnaire was being constructed, turned out to be the simplest way of identifying individuals for research purposes without revealing their names.

Omitting the siblings of the late-talking children from the close relatives whose occupations and music-playing were sought was another mistake. While this may be a minor omission in this first survey, when most of the siblings are too young to have careers, the siblings should not be omitted in later surveys, as they and the late-talking children continue on into adulthood. Since siblings are, biologically speaking, the closest relatives of all, their patterns are a major part of the family patterns. I also neglected to separate grandparents into maternal and paternal, so that when two occupations were listed on the line for grandfathers, for example, I had no way of knowing whether one grandfather worked in both occupations or each of the grandfathers worked in different occupations. This led to more phone calls.

A number of questions that were asked in an open-ended fashion could better have been presented as specific choices to be made by checking the appropriate boxes. For example, asking about the children's special likes and dislikes caused computers to be listed most often (13 times) but there is of course no way of knowing how many other parents would also have checked a box marked "computers" if there had been one. Nor can we know how many more parents would have checked music among the likes or noise among the dislikes. Open-ended questions about when the parents first became concerned about the child's late talking, or when the child became toilet-trained might better have been presented in terms of boxes marked in months. That way, a child for whom the appropriate answer is two years and ten months will not seem later to be so different from a child for whom the appropriate answer is three years and one month, for even though they talked or became toilet-trained in different years of their lives, these things occurred only three months apart from one child to the next. As regards toilet-training, this might be clarified in future surveys as daytime toilet-training, so that a child who wets the bed at night would still be considered toilet-trained if he used the toilets when awake.

Some questions, or the tabulations of the answers, need more clarification. Perhaps the most fundamental thing that should have been stressed was that the material in these questionnaires was going into a computer, so that (1) answers had to fit the categories given, since explanations, attached medical or other evaluations, or a redefining of the terms (expanding "accountant" to include bookkeepers or expanding the list of relatives to include cousins) represented things that could not be fed into the computer, (2) the particular question asked was the one to be answered, not some related question that might seem more interesting, and (3) the answers were not intended to help me diagnose individuals but to discern patterns in the group as a whole.

The question in section III of the second questionnaire that asked about the integration of speech with gestures and facial expressions seems to have been misunderstood by some parents, who reported on how their children used gestures or pantomime as *substitutes* for speech before they learned to talk. That is an entirely different phenomenon. What the question was trying to get at was whether the child's speech was accompanied by gestures and changing facial expressions, as with most people, or whether it was the kind of stilted, undemonstrative speech often found among autistic children. The first question in the same section asked when the child spoke his first word without making a distinction between something that may be merely a sound without meaning, such as "dada." When that same sound is in fact used by the child to indicate a parent, an object or something else, then it is a truly a word to the child.

The biggest disappointment among the answers to the questionnaires was the scarcity of mental test results. While this is not a deficiency of the questionnaire itself, future surveys should try to acquire this crucial information, even if that requires administering an IQ test to the children. Many of the parents, however, explained that they had sufficient confidence in their child's intelligence not to require formal testing.

Some questions should be dropped from the questionnaire as not very useful at all or as no longer useful after the first survey. The question as to whether there were more boys than girls, or vice-versa, in the families of the late-talking children was an attempt to see if perhaps other families in the group had a pattern similar to those among my siblings, where boys have predominated among the next generation. No such pattern was found. Other questions about early childhood history, or family history in general, need not be asked again, though the occupations of siblings or their music-playing should be asked about.

No doubt others will think of still more ways in which the questionnaires or the survey methods might be improved. I will gladly pass the torch to them on that, as on the other aspects of this research.

Index

abstract concepts, 38; inability to understand, 30, 66, 68

accountants, 82, 84

Adelaide, University of, 114

allergies, 39, 121, 123, 125, 137, 145–46

Amherst College, 13–15

Amy, 42–50

analytical ability, 77, 102, 103; brain factors in, 120, 123, 125; evidence of, in early childhood, 5; professions requiring, 82, 83, 98, 119

Andrew, 34–38

Andy, 73–75

artistic ability, 66, 67, 69

Asians, 83

Australia, 106–14

autism, 86, 95, 98, 105–14, 118, 125–26, 142*n*22, 146; evaluation for, 34, 45, 50–51, 65, 131; labeling of, and availability of services, 58–59; misdiagnosis of, 2, 17, 28, 29, 38, 42, 46, 54, 55, 67, 93, 125–26, 129; symp-

toms of, 43, 44, 50, 103; *see also* pervasive developmental disorder

Autism Research Institute, 53

back-and-forth conversation, 67–68, 73; age at achieving, 42, 80, 87

behavior problems, 63, 71, 74; *see also* tantrums

Billy, 52–62, 134

birth order, 119

Bishop, D. V. M., 117

blacks, 83

blindness, 61, 75–76; intelligence testing and, 131–32

boys, late-talking among, 2, 17, 18, 83–84, 100; brain factors in, 122–25; in institutional settings, 133

brain, 71, 120–28; early childhood stimulation of, 136–37

Brandeis University, 11

Bryan, 129

Bryant, Jean, 106–14